British
GARDEN LIFE

British
GARDEN LIFE

Written by:

Camilla de le Bedoyere

Miles
KeLLy

First published in 2007 by
Miles Kelly Publishing Ltd
Harding's Barn, Bardfield End Green,
Thaxted, Essex, CM6 3PX, UK

Copyright © Miles Kelly Publishing Ltd 2007

This edition printed in 2015

4 6 8 10 9 7 5 3

Publishing Director Belinda Gallagher

Creative Director Jo Cowan

Editor Amanda Askew

Assistant Editor Lucy Dowling

Cover Designer Jo Cowan

Design Concept Candice Bekir

Page Layout Stephan Davis

Picture Researcher Laura Faulder

Production Elizabeth Collins, Caroline Kelly

Reprographics Stephan Davis,
Thom Allaway

Archive Manager Jennifer Cozens

Assets Lorraine King

ISBN 978-1-78209-128-8

Printed in China

British Library Cataloguing-in-Publication Data
A catalogue record for this book is
available from the British Library

Made with paper from a sustainable forest

www.mileskelly.net
info@mileskelly.net

CONTENTS

TREES & SHRUBS

FLOWERS & GRASSES

CREATING A WILDLIFE GARDEN

Gardens, at any size, are home to many different types of creature, and with a little effort, it is easy to make a garden a welcoming place for many more.

TREES & SHRUBS

Many creatures need trees, shrubs and plants to survive. They use them for food, shelter and as a place to lay eggs and protect their young from predators. Trees and shrubs, such as hawthorn and bramble, produce berries and other soft fruits. These provide food for birds, which is especially important in winter.

- Avoid using chemicals, such as insecticides and herbicides, on plants as they can stay in the soil and harm the creatures you want to visit the garden, as well as those you don't.
- Avoid cutting plants back if they are providing useful shelter for animals.

- Encourage plants with flowers and fruits to grow by watering them and feeding them, as necessary.

▼ *Birds build their nests in tree boughs, where chicks are safe from most predators.*

FLOWERS & GRASSES

Flowers make pollen and nectar, which attract insects to the garden. The insects then attract birds and mammals. Most flowers and grasses are useful to animals, because they provide food and shelter.

▼ Bees are attracted to flowers by their bright colours, perfume and sweet nectar.

- A variety of flowers and grasses encourages the biggest range of wildlife. Some insects even prefer flowers of a particular colour.
- Flowers such as buddleia, Michaelmas daisies, sweet Williams and marigolds attract butterflies to the garden.

REPTILES & AMPHIBIANS

These creatures are shy and need plenty of vegetation to hide from predators. Amphibians need water to lay eggs in, and since the young live in water, too, creating a pond attracts them into the garden. Reptiles are rare visitors to most gardens, especially in towns and cities.

- If you don't have a pond, make a mini-pond by digging a tray into a garden bed. Add stones to help animals get in and out easily, and fill it with water.
- Old drainpipes or small shelters made from roofing tiles can become homes for reptiles and amphibians.

▶ Amphibians prefer damp habitats because they breathe through their moist skin.

BIRDS

◄ Nuthatches use their long, pointed beaks to prise nuts out of bird feeders.

Although birds need shrubs and trees to nest in, they will visit small gardens for food. During winter, when food is scarce, seeds and nuts put out on a bird table, or in a bird feeder, will tempt birds. They also need extra food in spring, when adults are feeding their chicks.

- Put a bird box in a tree to encourage nesting there. You can buy, or make, a bird box. Ask for an adult's help.

- Never disturb a nest. If an adult bird sees you near its nest, it may abandon its eggs or nestlings.

- Leave out nesting materials, such as feathers or wool, and birds may take them to build their nests.

- Make, or buy, a simple bird bath as birds need to drink and they like to wash themselves.

- Solid cooking fat and seeds in a yogurt pot can be hung from trees to encourage small birds.

MAMMALS

Mammals, such as foxes and rats, may not be welcome visitors to gardens. Others, such as hedgehogs, will hibernate and forage in piles of leaf litter. Never move leaf litter without checking if any mammals have made their home there.

- Make a hedgehog home by propping up a board against a wall or fence. Fill the space with dried grass and leaves.
- Ask an adult to help you to nail a box onto a tree for bats to roost in.

▶ *Squirrels can help trees to grow because they collect nuts and bury them in the garden.*

BUGS

Invertebrates, such as beetles and butterflies, will come into gardens if there are plenty of places for them to live. That means allowing areas of the garden to grow wild. Beetles often like to live in piles of rotting wood, and some butterflies lay their eggs on the underside of nettles.

- Make a log pile of old pieces of wood. Stag beetle larvae feed on rotting wood, and can live in a log pile for six years.
- Fill a shallow dish or container with small stones. Then add water to make a puddle. Watch butterflies as they come to drink.

▶ *Snails eat the leaves of many garden plants and, in turn, are eaten by birds, such as thrushes.*

HABITATS

The place where an animal or plant lives, feeds and breeds is known as its habitat. Some habitats can be created in the garden, encouraging wildlife to live there.

MAKE A BIRD BOX

Finding a place to build a nest is difficult for birds. Putting up a nesting box is a simple way to help birds find a home.

You will need:
plank of untreated wood, about 1.5 cm x 15 cm x 120 cm • screws screwdriver • two hinges • saw electric drill with a plug cutter

Ask for an adult's help to saw and drill the box, and to hang it.

1. Plan your box carefully on paper first. Decide how long your sides are going to be, as well as the base and the lid. The lid will need to overhang the box. Cut all your pieces of wood using the saw.

2. Using the drill and plug cutter, make the hole where the birds will enter the box. Use the screws to put all the pieces together, except for the lid. Attach the lid with hinges so you can clean the box out.

3. Bird boxes need to be hung high up in trees, where cats cannot reach them. They need a quiet place that does not get lots of strong sunlight as too much heat can kill chicks.

▶ *If you have a nesting box in your garden, you can watch bird activity more closely. Birds may start to regularly visit your garden.*

CREATE A POND

Ponds encourage wildlife to visit the garden. Many invertebrates live in water, and amphibians need water to breed. Birds and mammals need water to drink.

You will need:
pond liner • special plants (from most garden centres) rocks • spade • newspaper

Remember that garden ponds need to be fenced off to prevent young children from falling in.

1. Dig a hole about 50 cm x 50 cm x 100 cm. You need sloping sides, so frogs can climb in and out.

2. Lay newspaper and then liner in the hole, leaving extra to go over the edges of the pond.

3. Line the edges with rocks. Fill it with water, then add the plants.

▼ *Frogs sit motionless in ponds, waiting for flies or other insects to come close.*

BUILD A COMPOST HEAP

Compost is a mixture of rotting plant materials. It is used on garden beds to help plants grow because it is full of nutrients.

▼ *Plant matter in a compost heap decays (rots) over time.*

- Put waste plant material in a heap, or in a compost bin – use an old dustbin and put drainage holes in the bottom.

- Put your kitchen waste into the compost bin (but no meat or cooked vegetables). Grass and other plant cuttings can go in, too.

- Keep the lid on the compost to create heat and stop rats from getting in.

- Turn the compost over from time to time to help it rot evenly. If your compost is a heap, rather than in a bin, beware of small animals living there, such as hedgehogs.

BE A GARDEN DETECTIVE

Watching wildlife is usually very easy – all you need to do is sit still outdoors and be patient. However, there are some useful pieces of equipment and advice that will help you to get the most out of being a garden detective.

USEFUL TOOLS FOR DETECTIVE WORK

Binoculars
It is difficult to see the detail on a bird's plumage, for example, with the naked eye. Binoculars magnify, or make things appear bigger, and they are essential if you are serious about learning more about birds and small mammals.

Notebook and pencil
Sketching an animal, or plant, is a really good way of getting to know it because you have to look carefully at every detail. There are spaces in this book for you to record your notes and pictures.

Magnifying glass
Small invertebrates are fascinating, but many are too small to see easily. A magnifying glass gives you the chance to see their limbs, antennae and other interesting details.

Trowel
A small garden trowel is useful for turning soil over if you plan to search for invertebrates. Wear gardening gloves, too, so you can avoid any nasty stings or bites.

HANDY HINTS FOR DETECTIVE WORK

Check plants for signs of damage. If there are chunks taken out of leaves, or the leaves have changed colour before autumn, there may be invertebrates living on the plant and eating it. Snails come out at dusk to eat tender leaves, leaving tell-tale slime trails.

Look for holes in the soil. They may indicate where squirrels have been digging for food, or burying their stores for winter. Bigger holes may be the entrances to homes for small mammals, such as rabbits.

Explore the garden at different times of day. During the heat of a summer's day you may find buzzing, busy insects, but little else. Sit outside at dusk and you may see bats and birds swooping overhead.

Use your ears. Listen to the sounds in your garden and follow them. You will find insects, such as crickets, and learn more about bird song.

Look for signs that wildlife has visited the garden. Footprints left in mud, such as these badger tracks, help to identify which animals use the garden, especially at night. Also look for piles of feathers and faeces.

THE GARDEN IN SPRING

Spring is a time when days get longer and most things begin to grow. At the beginning of spring there is little sign of new life, except for the closed buds on trees and the first snowdrops. By the end of spring, the garden is green and busy with new life.

Blossoming trees
Some trees burst into blossom in spring, even before leaves have broken out of their buds. Insects emerge from hibernation, or from their eggs or pupae, to drink the sweet nectar.

Mad hares and songbirds
In March, hares can occasionally be seen boxing with each other before mating. Songbirds, such as nightingales, begin to prepare their nests for breeding.

Butterflies emerge
When the days are warm enough butterflies, such as the small tortoiseshell and brimstone, begin to emerge from their pupae. The peacock butterfly, recognized by the false eyes on its wings, is one of the earliest seen in spring. Before long, caterpillars will begin to feed on the new plants.

Snakes and lizards

Reptiles need the warm weather of spring to become active. By April and May, lizards and snakes are more visible than earlier in the year. They can often be seen basking in the heat of the sun on rocks or stones.

Frogspawn

The first signs of amphibian life appear when frogs mate and lay their eggs, or spawn, in ponds. The spawn is a jelly-like mass, with hundreds of small black spots – the developing tadpoles. Toads usually mate later in the year than frogs.

Early flowers

With a ready-made store of food, flowering bulbs, such as daffodils, start to produce shoots early in spring, long before other flowers bloom.

THE GARDEN IN SUMMER

Spring soon turns into summer, and it is impossible to say when one ends and the other begins. During summer, the garden is a busy place – flowers and trees bloom, and animals born in spring are now active, especially because food is in plentiful supply.

Hawthorn habitat

Between late spring and early summer, hawthorn bushes and trees come into flower, shortly after the leaves have appeared. The prickly stems make a perfect place for birds to nest, protecting the chicks from predators, such as cats. The flowers attract nectar-drinking invertebrates, such as bees.

Busy badgers

Badgers are now busy outside their setts, and hedgehogs begin their mating season. Hedgehog courtship can be noisy and their mating calls sound almost human.

Pond life

Ponds that once contained frogspawn now have plenty of tiny froglets leaping in and out of the water. Many tadpoles are eaten by other animals, such as fish, but enough survive to adulthood.

Fruits ripen

During summer, edible fruits, such as apples, blackberries and pears, begin to ripen. Some fruits fall from trees long before they are ripe, and are quickly eaten by small mammals and insects. Mice use their sharp teeth to eat fruits, such as apples.

Gardens bloom

In summer, flowers, from hollyhock to hibiscus, burst open to show their range of colours and perfumes. Garden flowerbeds and pots are full of daffodils and tulips, and woodlands are decorated by carpets of bluebells. Insects are attracted to gardens that are full of flowers as they feed on nectar.

Playful cubs

By June, the cubs of red foxes are brave enough to come into gardens and play. Their mother will be nearby, resting in the shade, watching her young.

Insects everywhere

Butterflies are seen mating, drinking nectar from flowers and resting in the sun. Peacock butterflies, for example, flock to the fragrant buddleia bush. Beetles scurry across soil and, at dusk, moths fly near windows, attracted to the light. Garden vegetables grow well in the heat, but they attract pests, such as aphids.

THE GARDEN IN AUTUMN

By September, the heat of summer has been replaced by a cool evening chill. The days are noticeably shorter, and mornings may be misty as often as they are bright. Growth slows down as animals and plants prepare themselves for the winter ahead.

Birds fly away

The cooler weather of autumn indicates to birds that it is time to move elsewhere. The birds that migrate to warmer countries for the winter begin to gather. Swallows flock together on telephone lines, and prepare for their long journey ahead.

Orb weavers

Spiders are busy throughout the year, but autumn is a good time to see their webs in full glory, as morning dew or mist hangs on the fine silk. Many creatures, such as flies, get caught in the threads.

Crane flies appear

In September, the sound of long-legged crane flies knocking against windows can be heard. These insects, also known as daddy-long-legs, hatch in September and huge numbers can be seen in gardens and parks.

Spotting shrews

After a busy summer spent eating insects, there is a larger number of shrews around in gardens and fields. Autumn is the best month in which to spot them, especially as many will not survive the coldest months of winter, as food is scarce.

Berries and fruit

By the end of summer, most fruits and berries have grown fat and juicy. They ripen and fall to the ground during autumn, where they rot or are eaten. Berries that stay on bushes until winter are eaten by birds because their other food source, insects, has become scarce.

Nuts ripen

Some trees produce nuts, which ripen in autumn. Many creatures take advantage of this new food supply, especially as flowers and fruits begin to die. Squirrels scurry up and down trees collecting nuts to store. They dig holes in the ground and bury the nuts so they can eat them later in the year.

Falling leaves

Autumn is also known as fall – the time when trees lose their leaves and become stark skeletons against the skyline. This is a good time to watch birds, as there are no leaves for them to hide behind. Tawny owls can sometimes be spotted at dusk as they prepare for night-time hunting.

THE GARDEN IN WINTER

Winter may appear to be a quiet season. Although it is a time for rest and recovery, there is still a lot activity. Many animals hibernate to avoid the coldest weather, but others remain active, trying to survive by finding new food sources.

The big freeze
A sharp frost, or heavy snowfall, may kill delicate plants unless they are wrapped in gardening fleece. Put a tennis ball at the edge of the pond when temperatures drop. You can take the ball out of the ice, leaving a hole so that animals can drink.

Snowtrails
On snowy mornings, trails left in the snow can reveal what wildlife is still in the garden. Footprints left by birds (shown below), foxes, feral cats, field voles and mice can all be identified. If you are unsure which animal the tracks belong to, take a photograph or make a sketch (with a scale) for identification later.

Unusual plants
Ferns, lichens (shown here) and mosses all thrive in the damp weather of early winter. They provide splashes of bright colour once the less hardy garden plants have died down.

Ivy flowers
When many plants have died down, ivy is still teeming with life. Ivy produces flowers as late in the year as November and, as so few other plants have any nectar, it is a popular place for many insects to visit. Small tortoiseshell butterflies may be seen drinking from ivy flowers.

Composts

In winter, many invertebrates struggle to survive in such low temperatures. They are also at a higer risk of being eaten by birds as food is scarce. Bugs living in compost, however, are warm and protected. Rotting matter creates heat, making compost a great habitat for insects and other invertebrates throughout winter.

Fungi and mould

The damp conditions of winter are perfect for the growth of mould and fungi. They are not true plants, since they do not use sunlight to make food (a process known as photosynthesis). They get their food by breaking down rotting matter.

Fox calls

During December and January, foxes begin to mate. Females (vixens) produce loud screams to let males know they are ready, and males bark in response.

HOW TO USE THIS BOOK

Use this guide to help you to find your way around this book. There's information about 100 different species of wildlife, amazing facts and measurements, and a photo file. You can add your own notes and pictures in the write-in area.

Photo File
See a close-up of each animal or plant in its natural habitat.

Fact File
Packed with essential facts and information.

Super Fact
Find out lots of amazing facts about each species.

Write-in area
Draw pictures and add notes, ideas and thoughts about anything you see.

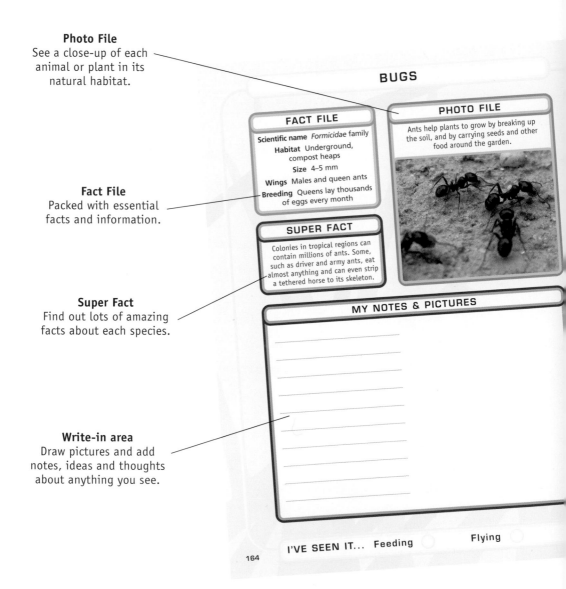

BUGS

FACT FILE

Scientific name *Formicidae* family
Habitat Underground, compost heaps
Size 4–5 mm
Wings Males and queen ants
Breeding Queens lay thousands of eggs every month

SUPER FACT

Colonies in tropical regions can contain millions of ants. Some, such as driver and army ants, eat almost anything and can even strip a tethered horse to its skeleton.

PHOTO FILE

Ants help plants to grow by breaking up the soil, and by carrying seeds and other food around the garden.

MY NOTES & PICTURES

I'VE SEEN IT... Feeding   Flying

164

22

The wildlife in this book is compared against something that you will know. This will help you to understand how big or small it actually is. The bugs, however, are shown at actual size.

 Human is about 1.8 m in height

 Cat is about 50 cm in length

ANT

Found in almost every habitat on land in the world, ants live in large colonies. They can be seen busily scurrying around a garden from spring to autumn, but are seen less often in winter when the temperatures are low. A colony of ants is divided into different types – the queen ant, female workers, and male ants. Some defend the nest, for example, while others are involved in reproduction.

ACTUAL SIZE

Main text
Every right-hand page has a main paragraph to introduce you to each animal or plant.

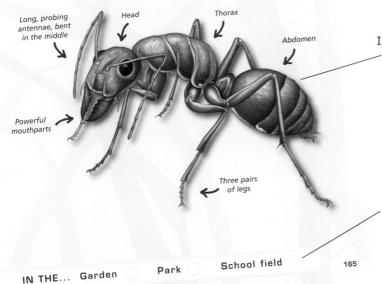

Long, probing antennae, bent in the middle

Head

Thorax

Abdomen

Powerful mouthparts

Three pairs of legs

Illustration
Images with labels to help you to identify each species.

Keep a record
Tick the circles to show what you've seen.

IN THE... Garden ◯ Park ◯ School field ◯ 165

TREES & SHRUBS

FACT FILE

Scientific name *Malus pumila*

Type Deciduous tree

Flowers White and pink, from spring onwards

Fruit Edible fruits containing seeds, from summer onwards

SUPER FACT

Apples were probably one of the first fruits to be grown for food, and they have been an important source of food in cooler countries for thousands of years.

PHOTO FILE

Apple trees are pruned (cut) regularly to help encourage the growth of flowers and fruit. A group of fruit trees is called an orchard.

MY NOTES & PICTURES

I'VE SEEN... Tree/shrub ◯ Flowers ◯ Fruits ◯

APPLE

Popular in many gardens throughout northern Europe, apple trees provide plenty of food and shelter for wildlife, including bugs and birds. Their tasty fruits can be eaten straight from the tree by humans, pressed to make juice and cider, or cooked to make sauces and puddings. There are many different varieties, or types, of apple tree. Bramley apples are larger than other varieties and are too sour to eat raw.

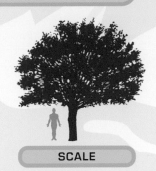

SCALE

Large, rounded crown

Tree shape

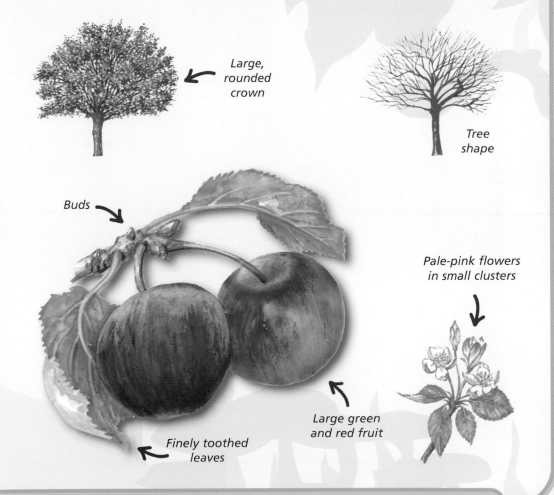

Buds

Pale-pink flowers in small clusters

Large green and red fruit

Finely toothed leaves

TREES & SHRUBS

FACT FILE

Scientific name *Rubus fruticosus*

Type Evergreen/deciduous shrub

Flowers White or pink blossom, from spring to summer

Fruit Green, ripening to red then black, from summer to early autumn

SUPER FACT

Bramble is closely related to the rose – it has sharp, curved thorns along its stem to deter animals from eating the fruits.

PHOTO FILE

The fruits, called blackberries, are green at first, but turn purplish-black as they ripen. They are then eaten by insects and birds.

MY NOTES & PICTURES

I'VE SEEN... Tree/shrub ◯ Flowers ◯ Fruits ◯

BRAMBLE

Also known as blackberry bushes, brambles have prickly, woody stems that can grow up to 3 m in length. Each stem can grow up or out, arching over other plants. Sometimes, the stems reach the ground where they will then grow roots. The flowers are pink or white, and appear in late spring or early summer. Bramble shrubs often grow up fences or walls, where they are protected from winds and bathed in sunshine, which ripens the fruits.

SCALE

Blackberries

Each tiny segment of a fruit, a druplet, contains a seed

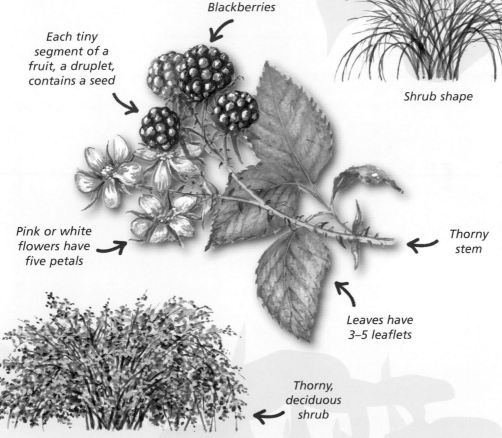

Shrub shape

Pink or white flowers have five petals

Thorny stem

Leaves have 3–5 leaflets

Thorny, deciduous shrub

TREES & SHRUBS

FACT FILE

Scientific name *Buddleia*

Type Evergreen/deciduous shrub

Flowers Lilac, white or pink, from summer onwards

Fruit Small fruits containing seeds, from autumn onwards

SUPER FACT

The butterfly bush got its Latin name, *buddleia*, from Reverend Adam Buddle (1660–1715) who was a keen collector of plants.

PHOTO FILE

Butterflies, such as small tortoiseshell butterflies, are attracted to gardens because they feed on nectar from the buddleia flowers.

MY NOTES & PICTURES

I'VE SEEN... Tree/shrub Flowers Fruits

BUDDLEIA

Often known as a butterfly bush, buddleia **can grow as tall as some trees, reaching more than 4 m in height.** It is a popular garden plant because it has attractive flowers with a strong scent, and is visited regularly by butterflies. The woody stems arch high, and have unusually shaped flower heads, called panicles. A panicle is actually made up of lots of tiny flowers, each with four small petals.

SCALE

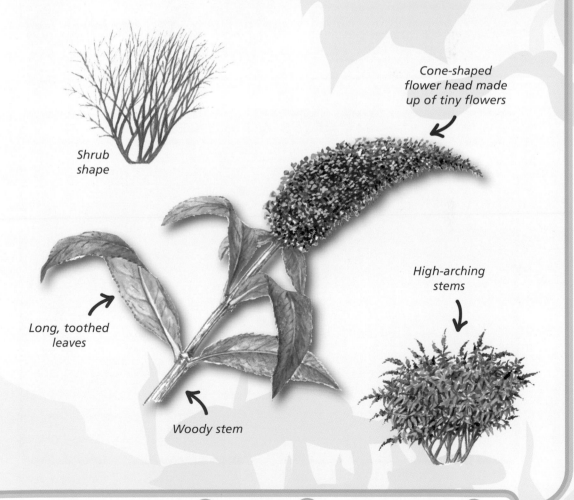

Shrub shape

Cone-shaped flower head made up of tiny flowers

Long, toothed leaves

Woody stem

High-arching stems

TREES & SHRUBS

FACT FILE

Scientific name *Rosa canina*

Type Deciduous woody shrub

Flowers Various, often pink or red, from late spring to summer

Fruit Hips are red or black, from late summer to autumn

SUPER FACT

Rose hips have unusual names, such as pixie pears and pigs' noses. They can be used to make teas, rich in vitamin C, by boiling them for at least ten minutes.

PHOTO FILE

Rose bushes rarely grow more than 2 m tall. The flowers can be various colours, but vibrant scarlet-red is very common.

MY NOTES & PICTURES

I'VE SEEN... Tree/shrub  Flowers Fruits

DOG ROSE

Roses are flowering shrubs that have been traditional garden plants for centuries, particularly in cooler climates where they thrive. Wild types, called dog roses, are most often found in hedgerows or growing along fences where they attract many insects and birds. Garden roses are normally grown for their beautiful flowers, variety of colours and strong scent. The stems are usually thorny, and the red fruits, called hips, appear in autumn.

SCALE

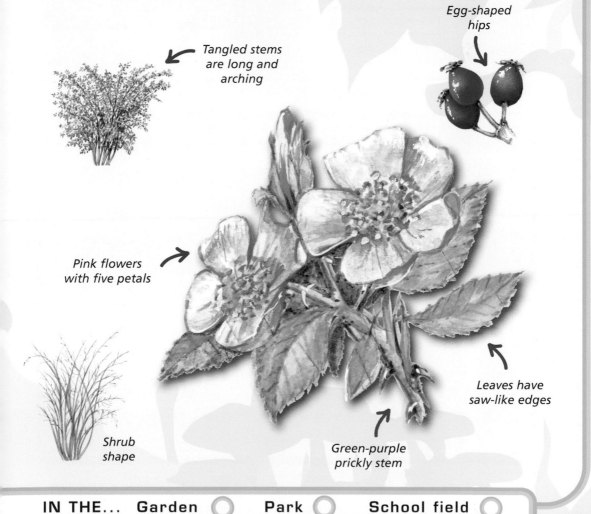

Tangled stems are long and arching

Egg-shaped hips

Pink flowers with five petals

Leaves have saw-like edges

Shrub shape

Green-purple prickly stem

TREES & SHRUBS

FACT FILE

Scientific name *Corylus avellana*

Type Deciduous tree or shrub

Flowers Yellow catkins, from spring onwards

Fruit Hazelnuts, from autumn onwards

SUPER FACT

Hazel sticks are long, thin and flexible. For thousands of years, they were used to make houses and they are still used to make fences and boundaries.

PHOTO FILE

Catkins are coated in fine, yellow pollen dust. The leaves are round with pointed tips and covered with soft hairs.

MY NOTES & PICTURES

I'VE SEEN... Tree/shrub Flowers Fruits

HAZEL

Hazel can grow as shrubs or trees, reaching **up to 6 m in height.** They are easy to recognize in the early spring, when the branches are draped in soft, yellow catkins, which are the male flowers. The female flowers are much smaller and look like buds. Later in the year, the ripe hazelnuts drop to the ground. Hazel leaves are sweet and tender, making them an ideal food for many caterpillars.

SCALE

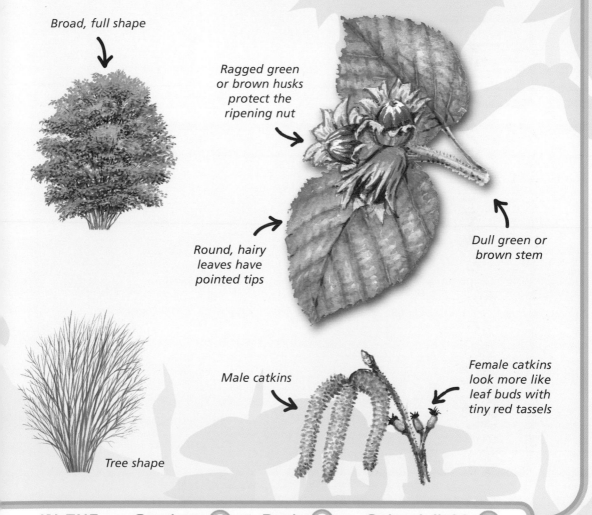

Broad, full shape

Ragged green or brown husks protect the ripening nut

Round, hairy leaves have pointed tips

Dull green or brown stem

Tree shape

Male catkins

Female catkins look more like leaf buds with tiny red tassels

IN THE... Garden ◯ Park ◯ School field ◯

TREES & SHRUBS

FACT FILE

Scientific names

Chive *Allium shoenoprasum*
Mint *Mentha* species
Parsley *Petroselinum* species
Rosemary *Rosmarinus* species

Flowers All summer

SUPER FACT

A herbal tea can be made by pouring hot water over a few mint leaves. Mint is said to help settle an upset stomach. Mint oil is used in toothpaste.

PHOTO FILE

The herb, mint, grows and spreads very quickly. It thrives in moist soil. When its leaves are rubbed, a strong minty smell is released.

MY NOTES & PICTURES

I'VE SEEN... Tree/shrub Flowers Fruits

HERBS

Many gardens have small areas for the cultivation of plants that are used in cooking. Mint, basil, rosemary, thyme, sage and chives are some of the most popular herbs. Many varieties of herb have been used for medicinal purposes, as well as for flavouring food. Herbs do not belong to one particular plant family, but they are normally small shrubs or tender-leaved plants. Not all herbs survive cold winters.

SCALE

Chive

Parsley

Rosemary

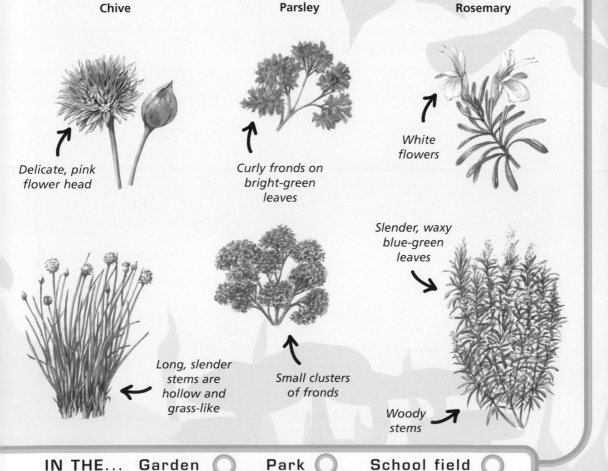

Delicate, pink flower head

Curly fronds on bright-green leaves

White flowers

Slender, waxy blue-green leaves

Long, slender stems are hollow and grass-like

Small clusters of fronds

Woody stems

TREES & SHRUBS

FACT FILE

Scientific name *Ilex aquifolium*

Type Evergreen tree or bush

Flowers Small and white, from late spring to summer

Fruit Red berries, from autumn to winter

PHOTO FILE

The distinctive leaves of holly are thick and waxy with spiky edges. The berries attract birds, such as redwings, blackbirds and fieldfares.

SUPER FACT

Holly berries are used as a Christmas decoration, particularly in wreaths. However, in cold weather, birds often strip the trees and bushes long before December.

MY NOTES & PICTURES

HOLLY

Throughout the cold winter months, holly is one of the few plants that provide colour. The deep-green leaves remain glossy and vibrant when so much else has died down, and bright-red holly berries attract winter birds to the garden. Holly can grow as a small, regularly pruned bush, or it can be allowed to grow into a tree reaching up to 10 m in height. Holly berries are poisonous to humans.

SCALE

Narrow, cone-shaped crown

Tree shape

Small scented flowers are white with four petals

Tough leathery leaves with wavy edges and sharp prickles

Scarlet-red berries

FACT FILE

Scientific name *Lonicera japonica*

Type Evergreen/deciduous shrub

Flowers Mainly white or yellow, from spring to summer

Fruit Red, blue or black berries containing seeds, from late summer to autumn

PHOTO FILE

There are more than 175 types of honeysuckle. They are all sweet scented and attract a huge range of insects, including bees.

SUPER FACT

The flowers and dried leaves of the Japanese honeysuckle, *Lonicera japonica*, have been used for many centuries in Traditional Chinese Medicine.

MY NOTES & PICTURES

I'VE SEEN... Tree/shrub Flowers Fruits

HONEYSUCKLE

A climbing bush, honeysuckle is often found creeping up walls and fences. Its pretty flowers have an unusual shape, but even more distinctive is the strong scent they produce. The nectar from these flowers attracts many insect visitors to the garden, including bees and butterflies. Honeysuckle grows quickly, producing many tendrils that cover fences, walls and trees. The leaves are favoured by many caterpillars and they often pupate (change from larva to pupa) amongst them.

SCALE

Berries ripen in autumn

Fragrant flowers are long and tubular, with sweet nectar at the base of each one

Bending, winding stems grow up and around other plants or fences

Pointed pairs of leaves

TREES & SHRUBS

FACT FILE

Scientific name *Hedera*

Type Evergreen shrub

Flowers Small, yellow-green, from late autumn onwards

Fruit Small black berries, from winter onwards

SUPER FACT

Although the black berries are an important food source for birds, they are extremely poisonous to humans.

PHOTO FILE

Ivy is known as 'lovestone' because it clings to walls, often covering buildings. In autumn, the leaves turn scarlet, pink or orange.

MY NOTES & PICTURES

I'VE SEEN... Tree/shrub   Flowers   Fruits

IVY

This shrub is usually grown in gardens as decorative cover, to hide fences and walls, or to provide a lush green carpet beneath trees where little else grows. There are many different types of ivy, but most of them have glossy, heart-shaped leaves. Shoots grow in all directions and many of them have tough roots to anchor new stems to the ground, or any other good growing surface.

SCALE

Small, black berries

Woody stem

Stems are covered in tiny roots that grow into soil, walls or fences

Flat leaves are dark green and glossy

TREES & SHRUBS

FACT FILE

Scientific name *Laburnum anagyroides*

Type Deciduous shrub or tree

Flowers Yellow, from late spring onwards

Fruit Brown pods containing seeds, from autumn onwards

SUPER FACT

The fruit is a pod, containing seeds. As the pod dries in the late summer or early autumn, it explodes open, throwing the seeds some distance from the tree.

PHOTO FILE

Laburnum rarely reaches more than 10 m in height. The bark is brownish-green and the hanging spikes are up to 25 cm in length.

MY NOTES & PICTURES

I'VE SEEN... Tree/shrub  Flowers Fruits

LABURNUM

A small tree, laburnum can be recognized by its hairy, green twigs. Also, in early summer, there are cascades of long hanging spikes of yellow flowers. Each flower on the spike looks like a small sweet pea flower. Laburnum is seeded very easily so it is found in many places, not just gardens. Every part of the plant is very poisonous to humans.

SCALE

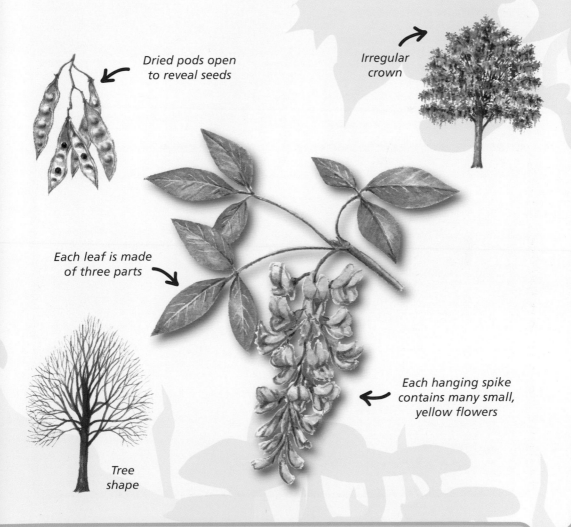

Dried pods open to reveal seeds

Irregular crown

Each leaf is made of three parts

Tree shape

Each hanging spike contains many small, yellow flowers

TREES & SHRUBS

FACT FILE

Scientific name *Lavendula*

Type Evergreen shrub

Flowers Small, lilac, from late autumn onwards

Fruit Small black berries, from winter onwards

SUPER FACT

Goldfinches eat lavender seeds, and use the dried stems to make their nests. Bees use the nectar to produce lavender-scented honey, which can be used in cooking.

PHOTO FILE

Every year, new stems grow from the tips of old, woody stems, so one bush can grow quite large over a period of a few years.

MY NOTES & PICTURES

I'VE SEEN... Tree/shrub ◯ Flowers ◯ Fruits ◯

LAVENDER

Strongly scented lavender bushes often feature as plants in garden beds, where the lilac flowers attract many pollinating insects. There are more than 25 different types of lavender, but they are all similar in shape and scent. The dried flowers are often used to flavour foods and perfumes, and may be added to pot pourris to keep clothes and bed linen smelling fresh. Lavender oil is often used in aromatherapy and traditional medicines.

SCALE

Small, lilac flowers

One stem carries many flowers

Thin, tough leaves

TREES & SHRUBS

FACT FILE

Scientific name *Sorbus aucuparia*

Type Deciduous tree or woody shrub

Flowers Creamy white, from May to June

Fruit Bright-red berries, from August to September

SUPER FACT

Rowan is believed to have magical properties and, in stories, is used to make magic wands. It is also said to give people psychic abilities.

PHOTO FILE

Rowan encourages wildlife. The leaves are a favourite food of many caterpillars and the berries are eaten by birds.

MY NOTES & PICTURES

I'VE SEEN... Tree/shrub Flowers Fruits

ROWAN

A small, hardy tree, rowan is easily recognized by its broad clusters of white, heavily scented flowers. It has narrow, oval leaves and in autumn, bears small, red berries. It is popular in gardens, but grows widely in parks and elsewhere. Rowan can grow as shrubs, but most European varieties are trees that reach up to 12 m in height. It is also known as mountain ash.

SCALE

Rounded, open crown

Orange-red berries

Small, white flowers in dense clusters

Saw-like leaf edges

Woody stem

Tree shape

TREES & SHRUBS

FACT FILE

Scientific name *Viburnum opulus*

Type Evergreen/deciduous woody shrub or tree

Flowers Small, creamy or green-white, from May to June

Fruit Red and blue-black, from autumn onwards

PHOTO FILE

Clusters of flowers are normally creamy-white although pink varieties occur. Each little flower has five petals and many types smell sweet.

SUPER FACT

A viburnum bush may grow several metres wide. It is an important source of food for garden wildlife, such as the viburnum beetle.

MY NOTES & PICTURES

I'VE SEEN... Tree/shrub Flowers Fruits

VIBURNUM

There are many different types of viburnum. The plant mainly grows as a shrub, although trees do exist. Most viburnums are deciduous and lose their leaves in autumn. This particular variety is often chosen by gardeners because the leaves turn a beautiful rosy red colour before falling. Viburnums that originate in warmer climates are often evergreen. The berries of some varieties are poisonous to humans.

SCALE

Tree shape

Reddish-brown leaves in autumn

Cluster of small, white flowers surrounded by larger flowers

Domed crown

Leaves are large with three lobes

TREES & SHRUBS

FACT FILE

Scientific name *Salix*

Type Deciduous tree

Flowers Male yellow catkins, from early spring, before the leaves fully open

Fruit Rare and small, containing seeds, from spring to summer

SUPER FACT

The bark has been used for medicinal purposes since ancient times. Experiments with a chemical from willow bark called salicin led to the discovery of modern aspirin.

PHOTO FILE

Weeping willows need plenty of water near their roots, and often grow along the sides of rivers, ponds and streams.

MY NOTES & PICTURES

I'VE SEEN... Tree/shrub ◯ Flowers ◯ Fruits ◯

WEEPING WILLOW

A large tree, weeping willow grows well near water. There are smaller varieties of willow that are more commonly found in gardens. Generally, weeping willows are one of the easiest trees to identify because they have long drooping shoots that can reach the ground. They produce yellow catkins on twigs that are often hairy. Leaves can be long and thin.

SCALE

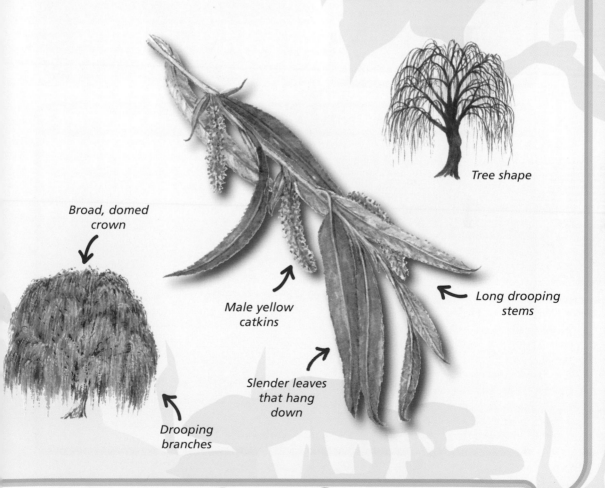

Tree shape

Broad, domed crown

Male yellow catkins

Long drooping stems

Slender leaves that hang down

Drooping branches

FLOWERS & GRASSES

FACT FILE

Scientific name *Phyllostachys*

Type Evergreen

Flowers Very rare, occuring every 28–120 years

Fruit Very rare, only occuring after flowering

SUPER FACT

Some bamboos can grow more than 30 cm in one day, although 3–5 cm is more likely in a garden. The hollow, woody stems were traditionally used as scaffolding.

PHOTO FILE

The tall, arching and slender stems of black bamboo are green when young, but after two or three years turn to ebony-black.

MY NOTES & PICTURES

I'VE SEEN...   Flowers   Fruits

BAMBOO

Although bamboo is a member of the grass family, it can reach the height of a tree. The stems, or culms, are divided into segments and the joints between segments are called nodes. They spread by means of rhizomes (underground stems from which roots grow) and a thick root system underground. There are more than 1000 different types of bamboo and they are popular garden plants because they grow very quickly, providing shade and greenery all year round.

SCALE

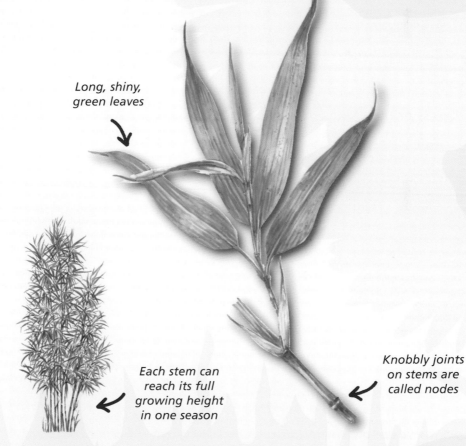

Long, shiny, green leaves

Each stem can reach its full growing height in one season

Knobbly joints on stems are called nodes

FLOWERS & GRASSES

FACT FILE

Scientific name *Convolvulus arvensis*

Type Perennial weed

Flowers White or pink trumpets, from May to September

Fruit Seeds (600 per plant), from August to October

SUPER FACT

Bindweed roots are fleshy and white. They grow extensively underground, and may grow down 5 m or more, making it very difficult to get rid of the weed.

PHOTO FILE

Bindweed is easy to recognize by its large white or pinkish flowers, and curling, thin green stems that wrap around other plants.

MY NOTES & PICTURES

I'VE SEEN... Flowers Fruits

BINDWEED

Although its white, trumpet-shaped flowers attract pollinating insects, bindweed is often an unwelcome addition to gardens. It is a weed that grows widely, climbing up fences and plants, gradually smothering them. Bindweed gets into gardens when plants are brought in, or through compost and manure. It can also spread by seed and is almost impossible to remove. Even a tiny piece of root can grow into a new plant.

SCALE

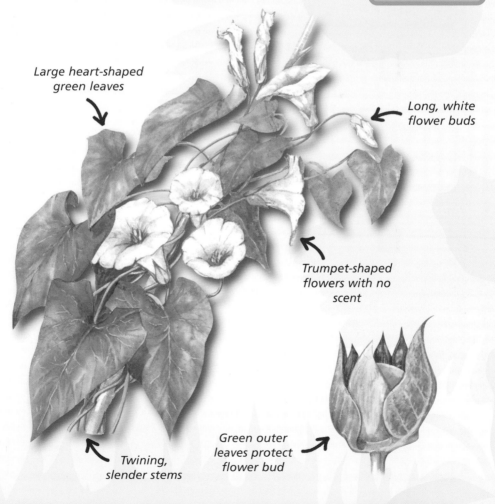

Large heart-shaped green leaves

Long, white flower buds

Trumpet-shaped flowers with no scent

Twining, slender stems

Green outer leaves protect flower bud

FACT FILE

Scientific name *Hyacinthoides non-scripta*

Type Perennial flowering bulbs

Flowers Violet-blue, from April to June

Fruit Seed pods when flowers die down

SUPER FACT

Bluebells contain a thick juice. It was once used to stick feathers on to arrows, bind the pages of books and make collars stiff.

PHOTO FILE

Thousands of woodland bluebell bulbs remain hidden from view underground, but in spring the flowers erupt into a carpet of colour.

MY NOTES & PICTURES

I'VE SEEN... Flowers   Fruits

BLUEBELL

When bluebells grow in large numbers, they create a carpet of dazzling blue flowers set amongst tall, green leaves. The flowers and leaves grow from bulbs in the soil. The bulbs store food, which means that the plants can start to grow without sunlight. Each flower head grows upright when in bud, but hangs down when it is in full bloom. Although bluebells may be found in gardens, they are also common in woodlands and hedgerows.

SCALE

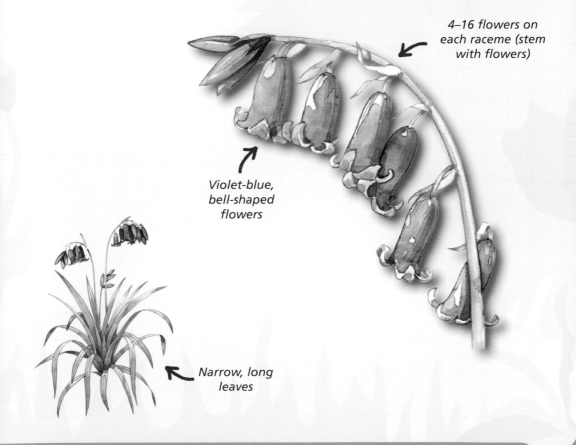

4–16 flowers on each raceme (stem with flowers)

Violet-blue, bell-shaped flowers

Narrow, long leaves

FLOWERS & GRASSES

FACT FILE

Scientific name *Clematis*

Type Evergreen or deciduous flowering climbers or vines

Flowers Various, from spring to autumn

Fruit Hard, dry seeds, from summer to autumn

SUPER FACT

The petals of a clematis are actually sepals (bud scales that enclose the flower) called petaloids. There are between four and eight on each flower head.

PHOTO FILE

There are more than 3000 varieties, or types of clematis. The flowers shown here have a delicate lilac colour and eight petaloids.

MY NOTES & PICTURES

I'VE SEEN...   Flowers   Fruits

CLEMATIS

Hundreds of different types of clematis **have been bred by gardeners around the world.** Most of them are climbing plants with attractive flowers and some have a lovely fragrance. They were originally grown as garden plants in Japan, but gardeners in Europe have been growing them for more than 500 years, producing a huge variety, including types that flower in early spring and others that are evergreen.

SCALE

'Fluffy' seed heads

Flower head has four petaloids

Leaf stalks curl around other plants as they grow

FLOWERS & GRASSES

FACT FILE

Scientific name *Bellis perennis*

Type Perennial flower

Flowers Small white flowers appear all summer

Fruit Tiny seeds, after flowering

SUPER FACT

Dried daisy flowers are used in traditional remedies for treating coughs and colds, diseases of the joints and minor wounds.

PHOTO FILE

Daisies are very common plants and grow not just in gardens but in all grasslands, meadows and by lakes and ponds.

MY NOTES & PICTURES

I'VE SEEN... Flowers Fruits

DAISY

The tiny white flowers that pepper garden lawns are called daisies and they are often regarded as weeds. The name, daisy, comes from 'day's eye' because the flower opens like an eye when the sun comes out. Daisies attract pollinating insects, such as bees and hoverflies. Their leaves are hairy and shaped like spoons, and the attractive flowers grow out of the centre of the plant. The plants survive cold and wet winters, and flower from spring onwards. The flowers grow upwards, facing the sun.

SCALE

Underside of petals are tinged with deep pink

Small, oval-shaped petals surround yellow disc

Straight, 'hairy' stem

FLOWERS & GRASSES

FACT FILE

Scientific name *Taraxacum officinale*

Type Perennial weed

Flowers Yellow, from spring to autumn

Fruit Tiny seeds with fluffy hairs, from summer to autumn

SUPER FACT

Dandelions get their name from the old French name for the plant, *dent de lion*. This means 'tooth of the lion' because the leaf edges look like a row of sharp teeth.

PHOTO FILE

Dandelion seeds are easily carried by the wind to new areas where they settle and can germinate – creating fields full of dandelions.

MY NOTES & PICTURES

I'VE SEEN... Flowers Fruits

DANDELION

One of the most common flowering plants, dandelions are found in gardens, parks and woodlands. They are considered weeds by many gardeners, but their bright-yellow flowers are a favourite of many pollinating insects. Other types of wildlife, such as rabbits, enjoy eating both flowers and leaves. The plants grow in a rosette shape, with the leaves and flower stem coming out of a central point, just above the tap root.

SCALE

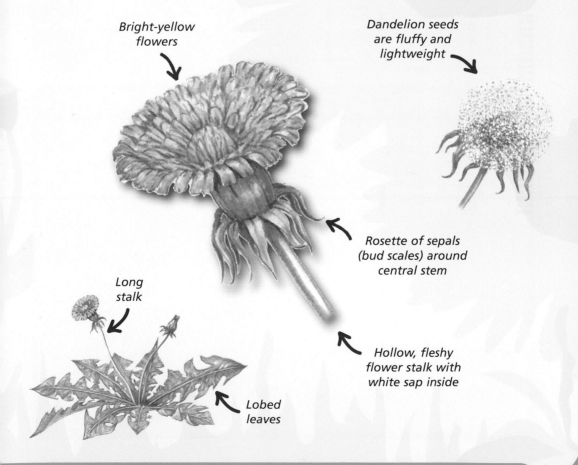

Bright-yellow flowers

Dandelion seeds are fluffy and lightweight

Rosette of sepals (bud scales) around central stem

Long stalk

Hollow, fleshy flower stalk with white sap inside

Lobed leaves

FLOWERS & GRASSES

FACT FILE

Scientific name *Digitalis*

Type Biennial flowering plant

Flowers Purple, pink, yellow and white, from late autumn

Fruit Small black berries from winter onwards

SUPER FACT

Foxgloves only last for two growing seasons. In the first season, the long leaves at the base of the plant grow, and the flower spike emerges in the second season.

PHOTO FILE

The pattern on the lower petal guides a pollinating insect inside to the nectar, while pollen brushes against the insect's back.

MY NOTES & PICTURES

I'VE SEEN...   Flowers ◯   Fruits ◯

FOXGLOVE

The common foxglove is one of Europe's most popular wild flowers. It is often grown in gardens for its tall flower spikes, which are full of attractive violet flowers. A single stem, or spike, can grow over 2 m in height, and is visited by bees and other insects. All parts of a foxglove plant are extremely poisonous, and even eating a small part can result in serious illness. The plants are not only poisonous to humans, but to animals as well.

SCALE

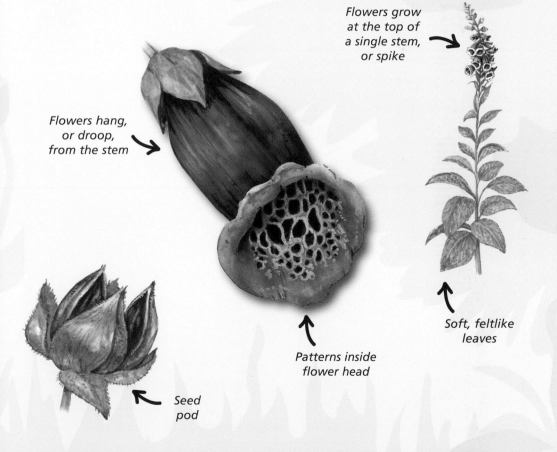

Flowers grow at the top of a single stem, or spike

Flowers hang, or droop, from the stem

Soft, feltlike leaves

Patterns inside flower head

Seed pod

FACT FILE

Scientific name *Pelargonium*

Type Perennial flowering plant

Flowers Red, pink, white, purple, from summer onwards

Fruit Small, oval seeds, after flowering

SUPER FACT

Pelargoniums were first brought to Europe from South Africa in the 17th century. Some types are grown for their perfume, especially those with a roselike scent.

PHOTO FILE

These pelargoniums have been grown in pots. They may be moved into window boxes to make a pretty display that lasts all summer long.

MY NOTES & PICTURES

I'VE SEEN...   Flowers ◯   Fruits ◯

GERANIUM

There are two types of popular garden plant known as geraniums. One type, called pelargoniums, are often used in window boxes, or as flower displays on patios. Although pelargoniums can survive drought, they do not cope well with frosts and rarely survive the winter outdoors. It is easy to grow these plants from leaf cuttings or small pieces of stem.

SCALE

Fruits, containing seeds, can only be seen when the petals fall

Trumpet-shaped flower heads

Large flower cluster on each stem

Large heart-shaped leaves

IN THE... Garden ◯ Park ◯ School field ◯

FACT FILE

Scientific name *Alcea rosea*

Type Biennial flowering plant

Flowers Purple, pink, yellow and white, from July to Sept

Fruit Large disc-shaped seeds, from late summer to autumn

SUPER FACT

In traditional Japanese festival dating back over 1000 years, people used hollyhock leaves to decorate cows and horses for a huge parade through the streets.

PHOTO FILE

Wild hollyhocks normally have yellow or pink flowers, but those that grow in gardens are usually white, dark plum or maroon.

MY NOTES & PICTURES

I'VE SEEN... Flowers ◯ Fruits ◯

HOLLYHOCK

Butterflies are encouraged into the garden **by hollyhock.** Many caterpillars like to eat the leaves, and adults can feed on the nectar. Hollyhock plants can reach up to 2 m in height, and have tall stems, or spikes, full of large flowers. The blooms can be used to create purple-, red- or rust-coloured dyes by simmering them in water to produce strong pigments that colour wool. Hollyhock may not survive for more than two or three years, but they produce plenty of seeds.

SCALE

Broad, flat leaves

Brightly coloured petals

Strong, upright central stem, 1–2 m in height

FACT FILE

Scientific name *Hosta*

Type Perennial flowering plant

Flowers White, pink or lilac, from summer onwards

Fruit Brown seed pods, from autumn onwards

SUPER FACT

Hostas, originally from China, are often eaten by slugs and snails. They feed on the leaves overnight, leaving only stems that are covered in tell-tale slime.

PHOTO FILE

Hostas have large elongated leaves that grow out of a central point. They can grow up to 40 cm in length.

MY NOTES & PICTURES

I'VE SEEN...   Flowers   Fruits

HOSTA

Also known as plantain lily, hosta is a **popular pot plant, and often features in garden beds.** They are grown for their attractive leaves, which are mostly green, or variegated (have mixed colours) with stripes of white and yellow, although some types have a bluish hue. Flowers bloom in summer but they are delicate and rarely have any scent.

SCALE

Bell-shaped flowers are white or lilac

Cluster of flowers on each stem

Long, upright stem

Leaves are long and shapely

FLOWERS & GRASSES

FACT FILE

Scientific name *Papaver*

Type Perennial flowering plant

Flowers Red, orange, white, blue and lilac, from May to July

Fruit Large seed heads containing tiny black seeds, from June to July

PHOTO FILE

Poppies are often found growing in meadows, fields and by roads. Their pretty petals are as delicate as tissue paper.

SUPER FACT

Poppy seeds have been used in cooking for at least 2000 years. They can be roasted or eaten raw, and are often added to bread, salad dressings and vegetables.

MY NOTES & PICTURES

I'VE SEEN...   Flowers   Fruits

POPPY

Garden poppies are often grown in flower beds and many types of poppy have been specially developed to produce big blooms. Some types of Oriental poppy produce large double blooms and a range of colours, including blue and lilac. Poppy seeds can lie dormant (resting) in the soil for many years, and only start growing when the soil is turned by a gardener.

SCALE

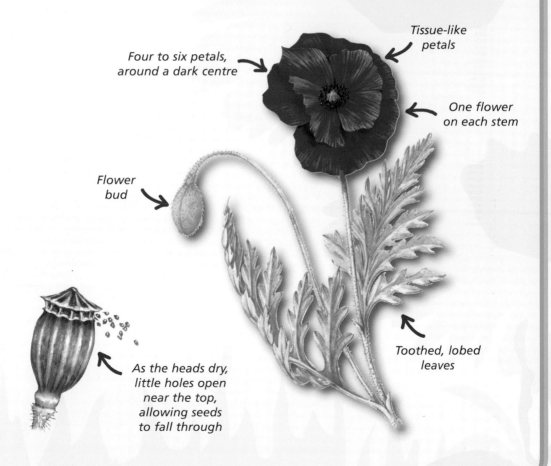

Tissue-like petals

Four to six petals, around a dark centre

One flower on each stem

Flower bud

Toothed, lobed leaves

As the heads dry, little holes open near the top, allowing seeds to fall through

FLOWERS & GRASSES

FACT FILE

Scientific name *Helianthus*

Type Woody flowering plant

Flowers Large yellow flowers with black or golden centres, from mid to late summer

Fruit Medium sized seeds, after flowering

PHOTO FILE

Sunflower seeds in the flower's centre are oval with black and cream stripes. They are favourite foods of mice and some birds.

SUPER FACT

Sunflowers are easy plants to grow. A single seed in a pot of compost will germinate in just a couple of weeks, if it is watered regularly and kept in a light place.

MY NOTES & PICTURES

I'VE SEEN...   Flowers   Fruits

SUNFLOWER

These tall flowering plants grow as a single stem with a huge flower head that can measure up to 30 cm across. A sunflower plant may reach 3 m in height. They are also grown by farmers as crops. The seeds can be eaten as a snack or added to cooking, but more importantly, they can be used to produce sunflower oil. This oil is used for cooking and as a fuel for cars.

SCALE

Yellow petals

Centre of flower head is packed with hundreds of seeds

Thick, hollow stem

Large leaves

Very tall stem

FACT FILE

Scientific name *Rana temporaria*

Adult size 6–8 cm

Habitat Shady, damp places

Hibernation November– February

Breeding Mating in spring. Eggs laid in still water

SUPER FACT

Frogs have long sticky tongues that they shoot out to catch flies and other insects. Frogs are friends to gardeners, as they also eat pests, such as snails and slugs.

PHOTO FILE

Adult frogs have smooth skin and long hind legs. The colour and pattern of their skin varies, but most are greenish brown.

MY NOTES & PICTURES

I'VE SEEN A...   Juvenile   Adult ◯

COMMON FROG

Found in moist, shady habitats, common frogs often live in gardens, especially where there are ponds, or in lakes or rivers nearby. Adult frogs come together in spring to lay their eggs in water. One female can lay up to 2000 eggs, called spawn, in a clump. Young, or juvenile, frogs are called tadpoles. They live in water until they change into adults. They can survive cold winter months by sleeping in mud at the bottom of a pond.

SCALE

Rounded snout

Large black eyes flecked with gold and brown

Forelimbs are shorter than hind limbs

Skin is moist and mottled brown and green in colour

Hind limbs have webbed toes

REPTILES & AMPHIBIANS

FACT FILE

Scientific name *Triturus vulgaris*

Adult size 7–11 cm

Habitat Damp places

Hibernation October–February

Breeding Mating in March and April. Eggs laid in still water

SUPER FACT

Females lay up to 300 eggs at a time on water plant leaves. Each egg is wrapped individually by a leaf for protection.

PHOTO FILE

Females are smaller than males and can be easily recognized because only males have a crest on their back and tail.

MY NOTES & PICTURES

I'VE SEEN A...   Juvenile   Adult ◯

COMMON NEWT

Newts are amphibians – they spend part of their lives in water, and part on land. These newts live in damp places in summer and survive cold winter temperatures by hibernating. They have a similar diet to frogs and eat insects, caterpillars, slugs, tadpoles and snails, which they hunt near water. Juveniles (young) breathe in water using their gills, but adults breathe using their lungs and moist skin.

SCALE

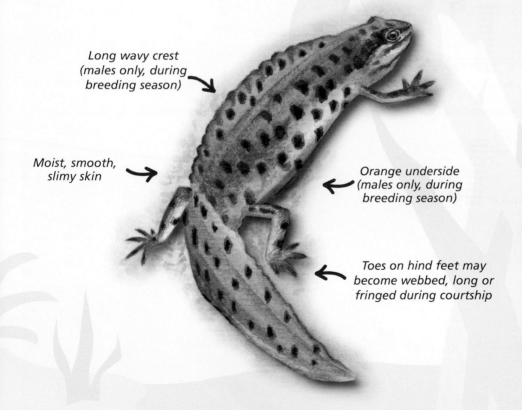

Long wavy crest (males only, during breeding season)

Moist, smooth, slimy skin

Orange underside (males only, during breeding season)

Toes on hind feet may become webbed, long or fringed during courtship

FACT FILE

Scientific name *Natrix natrix*

Adult size 1.2–2 m

Habitat Low-growing vegetation

Hibernation October–March

Breeding Mating in March and April. Eggs laid in rotting plants

SUPER FACT

If grass snakes are disturbed, they dive into water and hide amongst the weeds. They are excellent swimmers and can stay underwater for up to one hour at a time.

PHOTO FILE

In summer, females lay 8–40 eggs, often in compost heaps, rotting logs or leaf litter. The young look like adults, but smaller.

MY NOTES & PICTURES

I'VE SEEN A...   Juvenile ◯   Adult

GRASS SNAKE

These snakes are shy animals and it is rare to see them in gardens, even if they are present. Females are usually longer than males, and can reach up to 2 m in length. Grass snakes feed on a variety of animals, including mice, frogs, tadpoles, newts, fish and birds. They are excellent swimmers and spend much of their time in ponds and slow-moving waters.

SCALE

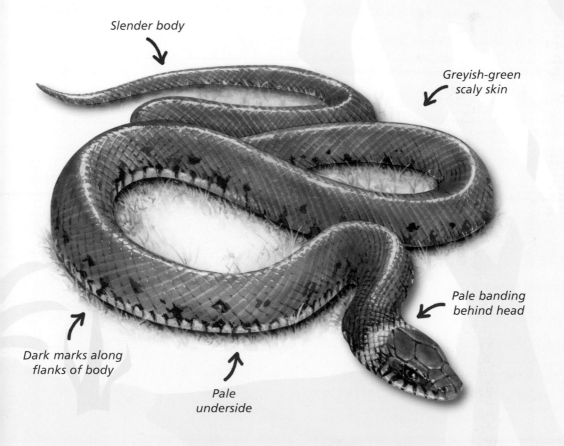

Slender body

Greyish-green scaly skin

Pale banding behind head

Dark marks along flanks of body

Pale underside

IN THE... Garden ◯ Park ◯ School field ◯

FACT FILE

Scientific name *Triturus cristatus*

Adult size 11–16 cm

Habitat Near pools and ponds

Hibernation October– February

Breeding Mating in March and April. Eggs laid in water

SUPER FACT

The tadpoles of the great crested newt look like adults, only smaller, when their legs have formed. They stay in water for four months before they can breathe air.

PHOTO FILE

Great crested newts are nocturnal and spend the day hiding among damp vegetation, in burrows and under rocks.

MY NOTES & PICTURES

I'VE SEEN A... Juvenile ◯ Adult ◯

GREAT CRESTED NEWT

Easily recognized by their colourful bodies, covered in warty bumps, great crested newts are large amphibians. The upper body is usually muddy brown, grey or black, and the underside is bright orange or yellow, and covered in black marks. Males have a long crest on their back and tail that grows bigger during the mating season. These newts prefer moist habitats, such as ponds, to dry places, but they are able to travel a short distance from water.

SCALE

Small head and eyes

Long jagged crest (in males only)

Orange skin with black marks

Dark brown skin, covered in warty bumps

White or blue streak on tail

REPTILES & AMPHIBIANS

FACT FILE

Scientific name *Lacerta vivipara*

Adult size 10–15 cm

Habitat Open areas

Hibernation October–March

Breeding Mating in spring. Young born from June onwards

SUPER FACT

Most reptiles lay eggs. Viviparous lizards, however, keep their eggs inside their bodies until they are ready to hatch. Between three and 20 eggs hatch in a litter.

PHOTO FILE

Viviparous lizards have good senses of sight and smell. They pounce on their prey, shake it to stun it, then swallow it whole.

MY NOTES & PICTURES

I'VE SEEN A...   Juvenile   ◯   Adult   ◯

VIVIPAROUS LIZARD

Lizards are reptiles and, unlike newts, can spend all their lives on land. Their skin is dry and scaly, and they often bask in the sun to warm their bodies. The viviparous lizard is also known as the common lizard. It has short legs and a very long tail, which may be twice the length of the body. The colours and patterns vary, but most are mixed shades of green and brown. Males are darker than females. These lizards are good swimmers.

SCALE

Dark stripe
down back
(females only)

Limbs positioned
on sides of body

Underside is pale
(may appear
orange in males)

Tail may be
twice the length
of the body

Dry, scaly skin

FACT FILE

Latin name *Tyto alba*
Size 30–35 cm
Wingspan 90 cm
Call Screeching and hissing
Breeding 4–7 eggs, from April to May. Chicks fly 8–10 weeks after hatching

SUPER FACT

Barn owls live alone, or in pairs. Males and females usually mate for life and both parents look after the chicks. They are rare and their nests must not be disturbed.

PHOTO FILE

Barn owls have large, heart-shaped faces, and are usually seen in open land, such as on farms and over fields.

MY NOTES & PICTURES

I'VE SEEN IT...   Eating ◯   Flying ◯   Nesting ◯

BARN OWL

Rare birds of prey, barn owls hunt for **their food at night.** Their bodies are covered in white and golden feathers. Like other owls, their eyes are on the front of their faces. They prefer open areas of land, but can be seen flying over gardens in the late evening, as they search for prey. Barn owls make their homes in sheds, church spires and natural holes in trees.

SCALE

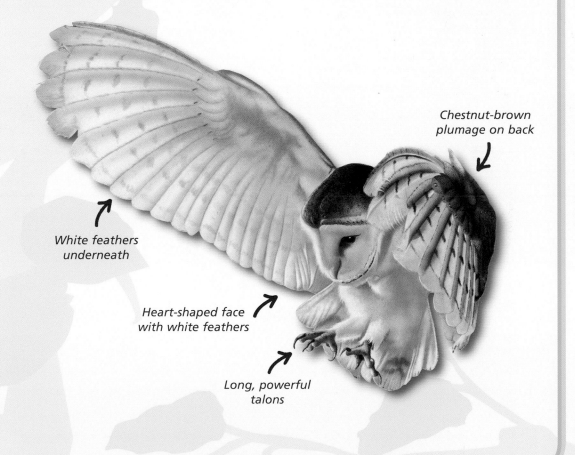

Chestnut-brown plumage on back

White feathers underneath

Heart-shaped face with white feathers

Long, powerful talons

FACT FILE

Latin name *Turdus merula*

Size 23–30 cm

Wingspan 35–38 cm

Call Flute-like and loud

Breeding 4–5 light-blue eggs with red spots, from March to April

SUPER FACT

Blackbird nests are made from grasses and lined with mud. The birds often build their nests in open, exposed places where birds of prey and cats may reach them.

PHOTO FILE

Blackbirds scour leaf litter and run across lawns looking for insects and worms. They also eat berries and fruits.

MY NOTES & PICTURES

I'VE SEEN IT... Eating ◯ Flying ◯ Nesting ◯

BLACKBIRD

Male blackbirds are unmistakeable visitors to the garden. They have all-black plumage, distinctive yellow bills and yellow rings around the eyes. Females, however, are harder to spot as they are dull brown all over, except for a paler streak on their throats. Blackbirds can often be seen hopping along the ground, looking for food. When they are alarmed, blackbirds have a loud and shrill call that sounds like a 'chack-ak-chack-ak'.

SCALE

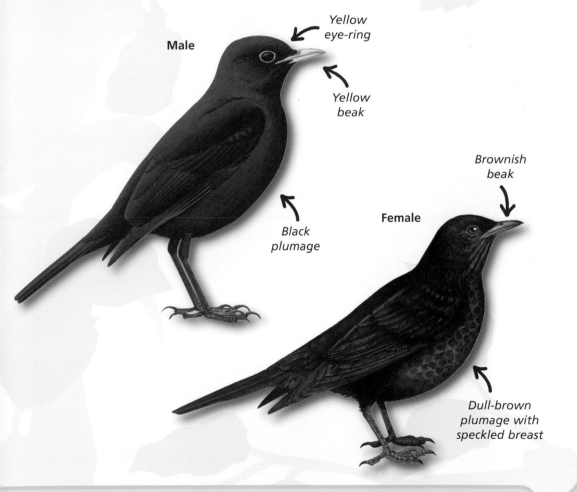

Yellow eye-ring

Male

Yellow beak

Brownish beak

Black plumage

Female

Dull-brown plumage with speckled breast

BIRDS

FACT FILE

Scientific name *Parus caeruleus*

Size 11–12 cm

Wingspan 17–20 cm

Call Clear and high-pitched

Breeding 7–12 white eggs with purplish spots, from April to May

SUPER FACT

Blue tits are popular because they feed on aphids. These are small insects that damage plants. They also eat other insects, including caterpillars, and nuts from feeders.

PHOTO FILE

Blue tits nest in holes in trees, walls and nesting boxes. The cup-shaped nests are lined with moss, hair or feathers.

MY NOTES & PICTURES

I'VE SEEN IT... Eating ◯   Flying ◯   Nesting ◯

BLUE TIT

Blue tits are small, lively birds and agile movers. They can hang upside down from twigs and bird feeders while eating, and can even perch on milk bottles to peck at the top and drink the milk. Blue tits have bright blue crowns and a yellow breast with a slight black stripe. Females have large clutches of eggs, and they have been known to lay as many as 19 eggs in a single clutch.

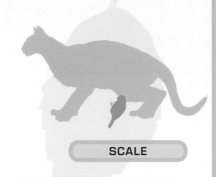

SCALE

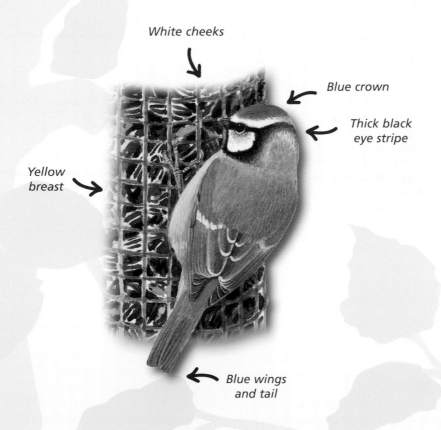

White cheeks

Blue crown

Thick black eye stripe

Yellow breast

Blue wings and tail

BIRDS

FACT FILE

Latin name *Corvus corone*

Size 44–50 cm

Wingspan 80–100 cm

Call Loud kraa-kraa

Breeding 4–6 blotchy blue-green eggs, from April to May

SUPER FACT

Animals that feed on dead bodies are called carrion eaters. Although these crows eat carrion, they also feed on eggs, insects and grain.

PHOTO FILE

Hooded crows are similar in appearance and lifestyles to their close cousins, carrion crows. Their plumage is mottled grey and black.

MY NOTES & PICTURES

I'VE SEEN IT... Eating ◯ Flying ◯ Nesting ◯

CARRION CROW

Both male and female carrion crows **have black plumage with stout black bills.** A close look at their feathers reveals a blue and purple shine, or iridescence. These crows live in a wide range of habitats, from gardens to coasts and mountains. Males and females share the job of building a nest, which is usually sited near the top of a tree, an electricity pylon or on a cliff edge.

SCALE

Black plumage with blue sheen

Small feathers at base of beak

Strong, perching toes with sharp claws

IN THE...   Garden ○   Park ○   School field ○

BIRDS

FACT FILE

Latin name *Fringilla coelebs*
Size 14–16 cm
Wingspan 24–28 cm
Call Loud trills and short 'pink'
Breeding 2–8 light-blue eggs in April, incubated for 11–13 days

SUPER FACT

Chaffinches build their cup-shaped nests with grasses, mosses and lichens in the fork of a tree. The nests are lined with feathers and joined with spiders' webs.

PHOTO FILE

Females incubate the eggs, but both parents look after the fledglings. After 11–18 days, the young birds leave the nest.

MY NOTES & PICTURES

I'VE SEEN IT... Eating ◯ Flying ◯ Nesting ◯

CHAFFINCH

Male chaffinches have rosy pink breasts and cheeks with bluish-grey heads. Females have greenish-brown backs and greyish-brown feathers underneath. Males and females both have brown beaks. Chaffinches have melodic songs, which differ from one region to another. They eat fruit, insects and seeds that they find on the ground, but they also catch insects in flight.

SCALE

Grey feathers on head

Male

Bands of white on wings

Pink chest feathers

Brown tail

FACT FILE

Latin name *Prunella modularis*

Size 13–15 cm

Wingspan 19–21 cm

Call Soft warble

Breeding 4–6 pale-blue, glossy eggs, from April to July, incubated for 12–14 days

SUPER FACT

Cuckoos often lay eggs in dunnock nests. The dunnocks are unaware that they are incubating an intruder, then the cuckoo fledgling throws the dunnock chicks out of the nest.

PHOTO FILE

Hedges are a popular nesting habitat for little dunnocks. They can often be heard singing from inside the shrubbery.

MY NOTES & PICTURES

I'VE SEEN IT... Eating ○ Flying ○ Nesting ○

DUNNOCK

Dunnocks are sometimes called hedge sparrows because at first glance they look very similar to the house sparrow. A dunnock's beak, though, is much slimmer than a sparrow's because it feeds on insects rather than seeds (stouter beaks are better at cracking seeds open). Male and female dunnocks look similar with ruddy brown streaking and pink legs, although the females are a little duller.

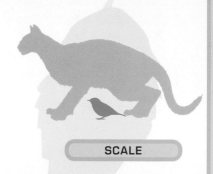

SCALE

Slender beak

Speckled feathers on back

Blue-grey head and breast

Pink legs

FACT FILE

Latin name *Turdus pilaris*
Size 22–27 cm
Wingspan 39–42 cm
Call Loud 'chack-chack'
Breeding 5–6 pale-blue eggs
with red speckles, from
April to July

PHOTO FILE

Fieldfares feed on seeds, berries and insects, including snails and worms. Hawthorn hedges laden with berries are favourite feeding areas.

SUPER FACT

Fieldfares migrate to the UK in winter, but they spend the rest of the year in Scandinavia where they breed. Nowadays, fewer fieldfares are seen in the UK.

MY NOTES & PICTURES

I'VE SEEN IT... Eating ◯   Flying ◯   Nesting ◯

FIELDFARE

One of the largest types of thrush, fieldfares are social birds. They are often seen hopping along the ground. They visit gardens when they cannot find food in open fields and hedgerows. During autumn and winter, they can occasionally be seen eating ripe fruit that has fallen from trees. Fieldfares usually feed, fly and roost together in flocks.

SCALE

Blue-grey head

Chestnut back

Yellow, thin, short beak

Black tail

Yellow-streaked breast with black patches

FACT FILE

Latin name *Sylvia borin*
Size 14 cm
Wingspan 20–22 cm
Call Melodic song
Breeding 3–7 dull-cream eggs
with grey spots, from
late May to June

SUPER FACT

There are about 400 different types
of warbler, and many are dull in
appearance. They are well-known
for their melodious singing.

PHOTO FILE

Garden warblers have keen eyesight to
spot small prey, such as ants and earwigs,
that scurry through leaf litter.

MY NOTES & PICTURES

I'VE SEEN IT... Eating Flying Nesting ◯

GARDEN WARBLER

Despite their name, garden warblers prefer woodland to gardens, although they do visit gardens with mature trees. They are migrants, and only come to the UK in summer, arriving in April and leaving in the middle of July. Their plain appearance helps to camouflage them, and they spend a lot of time in bushes and hedgerows searching for insects and berries to eat.

SCALE

Small, slender beak

Olive-brown plumage

Paler colour underneath

FACT FILE

Latin name *Carduelis carduelis*
Size 12 cm
Wingspan 21–25 cm
Call Soft twills and twitters
Breeding 4–7 speckled blue eggs, from May to August

PHOTO FILE

Goldfinches love seeds and they can often be seen near sunflowers, thistles, dandelions, teasels and bird-feeders.

SUPER FACT

It was once fashionable to have caged birds in the home, and goldfinches were a favourite because of melodious song.

MY NOTES & PICTURES

I'VE SEEN IT... Eating ◯ Flying ◯ Nesting ◯

GOLDFINCH

Distinctive visitors to the garden, goldfinches are easy to identify. Males and females look alike – they have red faces with white cheeks and throats. The top of the head is black, and the wings have broad yellow bands. In winter, many goldfinches migrate south to warmer weather, returning in March and April, but some choose to stay in the UK all year round.

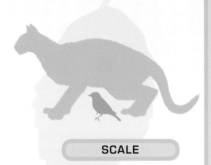

SCALE

Pinkish beak

Red, black and white face

Brown back

Golden bars on black-and-brown wings

White feathers underneath

FACT FILE

Scientific name *Dendrocopos major*

Size 22–33 cm

Wingspan 34–42 cm

Call Sharp, short 'tchak'

Breeding 4–7 white eggs, from April to June

PHOTO FILE

Woodpeckers visit large gardens in search of insects or seeds and nuts. They are shy and easily scared.

SUPER FACT

Woodpeckers make a characteristic drumming noise with their beaks on trees. They look for bugs in the cracks in bark. They have very long tongues for picking up food.

MY NOTES & PICTURES

I'VE SEEN IT... Eating   Flying Nesting

GREAT SPOTTED WOODPECKER

Boldly coloured, great spotted **woodpeckers are black and white, with red rumps.** Males also have a red splash on the nape of the neck. Youngsters look similar, but the colours are less bold. They are the size of a blackbird, and the largest of the woodpeckers found in the UK. They live in woodlands, parks and gardens with large trees and scurry across tree trunks looking for insects to eat.

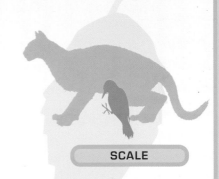

SCALE

Pointed beak

Red mark on back of head

Red undertail

White bands on wings

BIRDS

FACT FILE

Latin name *Carduelis chloris*
Size 15 cm
Wingspan 25–28 cm
Call Wheezy song with whistles and twitters
Breeding 4–6 speckled cream eggs, from April to May

SUPER FACT

Greenfinches are common in gardens, where they can find food easily. They like peanuts and sunflower seeds in particular.

PHOTO FILE

Greenfinches can be confused with siskins, which also have yellow-green bodies. However, greenfinches do not have black caps or bibs.

MY NOTES & PICTURES

I'VE SEEN IT... Eating ◯   Flying ◯   Nesting ◯

GREENFINCH

Greenfinches are stout birds that **often live in groups in hedges and other dense vegetation.** Their bodies are mostly green, with yellow bands on their wings. Females and males look similar, but the females have more brown in their plumage. Greenfinches often come together in groups, or colonies, at breeding time. When the juveniles have left the nest, greenfinches may travel south for the winter.

SCALE

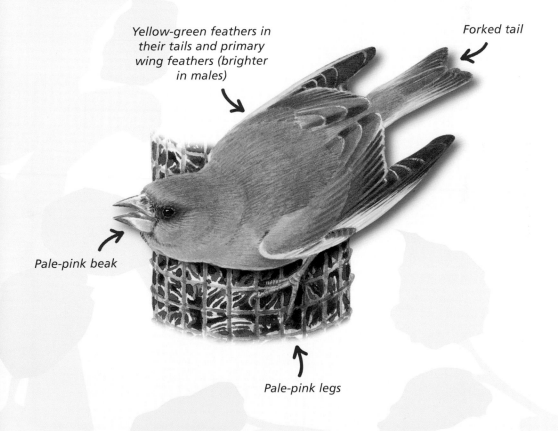

Yellow-green feathers in their tails and primary wing feathers (brighter in males)

Forked tail

Pale-pink beak

Pale-pink legs

BIRDS

FACT FILE

Latin name *Delichon urbica*
Size 12–15 cm
Wingspan 25–30 cm
Call Twittering
Breeding 4–5 white eggs, from May to August

SUPER FACT

House martins are occasionally attracted to hot air balloons. They fly in circles above the balloons, maybe enjoying a free ride on the rising current of warm air.

PHOTO FILE

House martins often make their homes near people, building nests under the eaves (where a roof overhangs a wall) of houses and sheds.

MY NOTES & PICTURES

I'VE SEEN IT... Eating Flying Nesting

HOUSE MARTIN

Often mistaken for swallows, house martins are actually smaller, have shorter tail forks and a white chin. They feed on flying insects, swooping over water or farmland to catch their prey. House martins are rarely seen on land, although they may be spotted over the garden at dusk. They often live in gardens with muddy pools, since they make their nests from mud. These summer birds migrate to warm countries in October, returning in spring.

SCALE

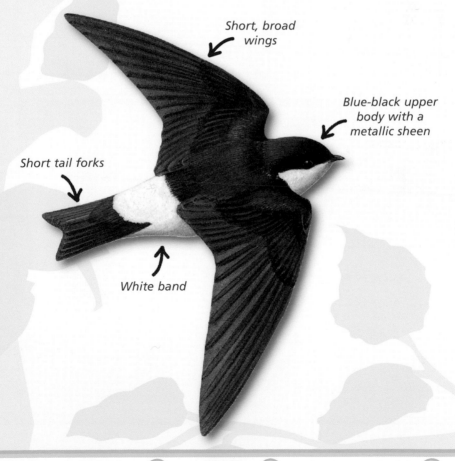

Short, broad wings

Blue-black upper body with a metallic sheen

Short tail forks

White band

BIRDS

FACT FILE

Latin name *Corvus monedula*

Size 33 cm

Wingspan 65–75 cm

Call Harsh calls, 'tchak'

Breeding 4–6, pale blue eggs in April, incubated by female

SUPER FACT

Rooks, carrion crows and jackdaws can easily be mistaken for one another. This rook has a longer beak than the jackdaw, and it is a larger bird.

PHOTO FILE

Jackdaws are mostly black, but have paler feathers on the back of their heads and necks. Their eyes are almost white.

MY NOTES & PICTURES

I'VE SEEN IT... Eating ◯   Flying ◯   Nesting ◯

JACKDAW

Small members of the crow family, jackdaws can survive in many different types of habitat, and eat a wide variety of food. They usually live and roost in large groups, or colonies. They make their nests in a variety of places including rock faces, chimneys, churches and natural holes in trees. Jackdaws prey on the eggs and fledglings of wood pigeons and other birds. They also eat insects, worms and will forage on rubbish dumps.

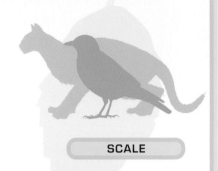

SCALE

White eyes

Paler feathers on neck

Black, glossy plumage

Grey underparts

IN THE... Garden ◯   Park ◯   School field ◯

BIRDS

FACT FILE

Latin name *Garrulus glandarius*

Size 31–35 cm

Wingspan 54–59 cm

Call Loud and harsh screech

Breeding 3–10 pale-green speckled eggs, from April to July

SUPER FACT

Jays feed on acrorns. They bury up to 3000 acorns in one month. They sometimes forget about them, so the acorns grow into trees.

PHOTO FILE

The jay has streaked feathers on its head. The feathers can be raised as a crest when the bird is nervous or scared.

MY NOTES & PICTURES

I'VE SEEN IT... Eating   Flying   Nesting

JAY

These birds are members of the crow family but, unlike most of their relatives, they have colourful plumage. Their bodies are pinky-brown, and the streaked feathers form a crest on the head. There are distinctive blue flashes on the wings and the eyes are pale. Jays are sociable birds, and males and females often stay together for life. They can copy the calls of other birds, but they often make a loud screeching noise when they arrive in a garden.

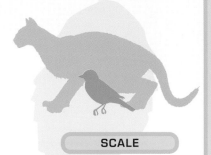

SCALE

Pinkish-brown body

Blue feathers on wing

Pink legs

White flash on the rump

FACT FILE

Latin name *Pica pica*

Size 41–51 cm

Wingspan 50–60 cm

Call Loud and harsh 'chacka chacka'

Breeding 5–8 glossy, spotted eggs, from April to May

SUPER FACT

Magpies are believed to bring bad luck. However, saying 'Good morning Mr Magpie' when you see one is supposed to ward off evil!

PHOTO FILE

Magpies are omnivores – they eat both meat and plants. Their diet includes rubbish, carrion, fruit, seeds, eggs and nestlings.

MY NOTES & PICTURES

I'VE SEEN IT...   Eating ◯   Flying ◯   Nesting ◯

MAGPIE

Large black-and-white birds, magpies **have very long tails.** In fact, their tails are longer than their bodies, particularly in males, and tinged with green. Magpies are most common in rural areas, especially near farms, but they often visit gardens and parks where they feed on rubbish and scraps. In spring, magpies can come together in large flocks called parliaments. They are often blamed for eating the eggs and nestlings of songbirds.

SCALE

Dark-coloured head

Glossy, metallic-blue feathers

Long tail with rounded tip

White feathers underneath

FACT FILE

Scientific name *Sitta europaea*

Size 11–15 cm

Wingspan 20–25 cm

Call Loud piping notes

Breeding 6–9 white eggs, from April to May

SUPER FACT

Nuthatches are easily mistaken for woodpeckers as they both perch on the bark of trees. Nuthatches, however, are the only birds that run headfirst down a tree.

PHOTO FILE

Nuthatches visit bird tables and seed feeders. They wedge nuts into cracks in trees and hammer them open with their beaks.

MY NOTES & PICTURES

I'VE SEEN IT... Eating ○   Flying ○   Nesting ○

NUTHATCH

Unusual looking birds, nuthatches are often seen running up and down the trunk of a tree searching for insects. They use their sharp, pointed beaks to search cracks in tree bark for bugs or seeds. Males and females look similar, but the colours are slightly darker in males. They live in woodlands, but often visit gardens in search of nuts and seeds.

SCALE

Orange feathers underneath

Large head with very short neck

Long, black eye stripe

White cheeks and throat

BIRDS

FACT FILE

Scientific name *Motacilla alba*

Size 17–20 cm

Wingspan 25–30 cm

Call Twittering song

Breeding 4–6 white eggs with grey spots, from April to June

SUPER FACT

Pied wagtails are often mistaken for young magpies, but they can be distinguished by their bouncing tails.

PHOTO FILE

A male's summer plumage is jet black on its crown, back, tails and wings. Plumage is greyer in winter.

MY NOTES & PICTURES

I'VE SEEN IT... Eating ◯ Flying ◯ Nesting ◯

PIED WAGTAIL

These birds visit gardens, parks and open fields, often near water. Pied wagtails are comical birds, often seen running quickly across the ground pausing only to look at the ground and wag their tails up and down. Although the plumage of pied wagtails is black and white, the actual patterns and depth of colour varies over the year. Females have more grey than black feathers. Pied wagtails usually eat insects.

SCALE

Black eye

White bars on wing feathers

Long tail that constantly moves

White feathers

FACT FILE

Scientific name *Erithacus rubecula*

Size 12–15 cm

Wingspan 20–22 cm

Call Warbling song

Breeding 5–6 white eggs, speckled with red, from March to July

SUPER FACT

Robins do not migrate from the UK, but in winter, robins from colder countries often migrate to the UK. They have paler breasts and are less tame.

PHOTO FILE

Juvenile (young) robins do not have red breasts. It is thought that this stops adults fighting with them for territory or food.

MY NOTES & PICTURES

I'VE SEEN IT... Eating ◯ Flying ◯ Nesting ◯

ROBIN

One of the most easily recognized garden birds, robins are dainty, with plump bodies and red breasts. The back is brown and the underneath is white. They are known as gardeners' friends as they often perch nearby when soil is being dug over, and they quickly leap on any insects that are exposed. Males and females look similar. Robins are associated with holly berries, not only because of Christmas, but also because in winter, when food is scarce, robins feed on the berries.

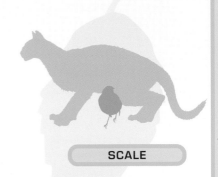

SCALE

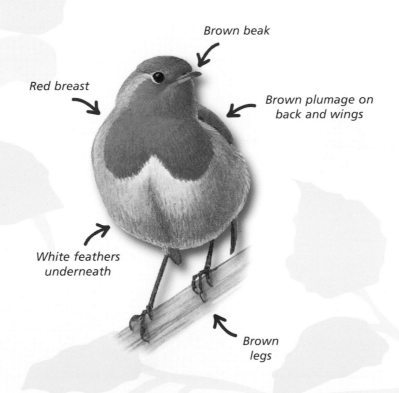

Brown beak

Red breast

Brown plumage on back and wings

White feathers underneath

Brown legs

FACT FILE

Scientific name *Turdus philomelos*

Size 23 cm

Wingspan 33–36 cm

Call Loud, clear and flute-like

Breeding 4–6 pale-blue eggs, from March to August

SUPER FACT

Thrushes build cup-shaped nests made from grasses and twigs. The inside is lined with mud and rotting wood, and stuck together with saliva.

PHOTO FILE

To feed on a snail, a thrush holds it in its beak and smashes it against a stone, breaking the shell. The bird can then eat the soft body inside.

MY NOTES & PICTURES

I'VE SEEN IT... Eating ◯   Flying ◯   Nesting ◯

SONG THRUSH

Often seen darting around between bushes, song thrushes use their ears and eyes to search for small insects or worms to eat. They have brown backs and pale, creamy-white speckled chests. Males and females look similar. Song thrushes live in woodlands, gardens and fields. They nest in trees, bushes and even garden sheds.

SCALE

Large eyes

Brown back

Speckled, cream breast

FACT FILE

Scientific name *Passer domesticus*

Size 14–15 cm

Wingspan 20–25 cm

Call Chirps

Breeding 3–5 pale-blue eggs
with grey blotches,
from April to June

SUPER FACT

The house sparrow is becoming
increasingly rare and has
disappeared from some parts of
the UK. No one knows for sure
why their numbers are falling.

PHOTO FILE

Sparrows like living near people, and large
flocks may nest or feed near parks and houses.
They feed on seeds, grain and insects.

MY NOTES & PICTURES

I'VE SEEN IT... Eating ◯ Flying ◯ Nesting ◯

SPARROW

Small, active birds, sparrows are a familiar sight in the garden. Males have grey caps and chests, and a bold black patch on the throat and upper chest. They also have a black eye stripe. Females are much duller in colour with a chestnut-coloured stripe over their eyes. Their nests are made from straw and grasses, and lined with feathers.

SCALE

Grey cap

Yellow-brown beak in winter (black in summer)

Chestnut-brown plumage on back is darkly streaked

Black throat patch and eye stripe

Grey breast

Pale brown legs

BIRDS

FACT FILE

Scientific name *Muscicapa striata*

Size 13–15 cm

Wingspan 23–25 cm

Call Soft but scratchy song

Breeding 4–5 pale-blue eggs, from May to June

SUPER FACT

The number of spotted flycatchers has dropped dramatically in recent years, and they are now a threatened species of bird. This may be due to a loss of habitat.

PHOTO FILE

Spotted flycatchers are often seen sitting upright on fences, posts or branches, before darting off to snap up passing insects.

MY NOTES & PICTURES

I'VE SEEN IT... Eating ◯   Flying ◯   Nesting ◯

SPOTTED FLYCATCHER

Slim birds, spotted flycatchers have grey-brown backs and pale underbodies. Their eyes, beaks and legs are black. When they perch, spotted flycatchers flick their wings and tail. They can be found in habitats where there are trees, including gardens, parks and woodlands. These fast-flying birds catch their prey while on the wing. Damselflies and butterflies are two of their favourite prey.

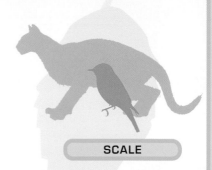

SCALE

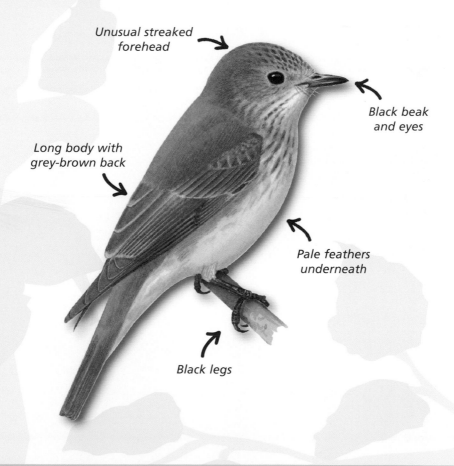

Unusual streaked forehead

Black beak and eyes

Long body with grey-brown back

Pale feathers underneath

Black legs

IN THE... Garden ⬭ Park ⬭ School field ⬭

BIRDS

FACT FILE

Scientific name *Sturnus vulgaris*

Size 19–22 cm

Wingspan 37–43 cm

Call Twitters, clicks and whistles

Breeding 5–7 pale-blue eggs, from April to May

SUPER FACT

Starlings are mimics – they can learn the songs of other birds and copy them. They don't stop at birdsong – they can also imitate car alarms and ring tones!

PHOTO FILE

Chicks feed on insects and larvae. They leave the nest after about three weeks, but are fed for a while after until they are independent.

MY NOTES & PICTURES

I'VE SEEN IT... Eating ◯ Flying ◯ Nesting ◯

STARLING

These birds have a reputation as one of the noisiest visitors to the garden. This is partly because they prefer to live and feed in large groups. These flocks are an amazing sight as they swoop into parkland or circle above a garden looking for suitable perches. Starlings are medium-sized birds that hold their bodies upright as they busily march around looking for food. Their diet includes insects, worms, seeds and scraps. Flocks of starlings were once common in towns but numbers have dropped recently as there are fewer places to roost.

SCALE

Slender, yellow beak

Small, light-coloured flecks on body and wings

Pointed wings

Metallic green-and-purple sheen on feathers

Short tail

IN THE... Garden ◯   Park ◯   School field ◯

FACT FILE

Scientific name *Hirundo rustica*

Size 17–22 cm

Wingspan 30–35 cm

Call Rapid twitter

Breeding 4–5 eggs with white spots, from April to August

SUPER FACT

Farmers avoid destroying swallow nests because the birds are thought to bring good luck. Swallows use second-hand nests – some are more than 50 years old.

PHOTO FILE

Swallows build their nests in sheds, buildings and porches. The nests are cup-shaped and built from mud and lined with straw or grass.

MY NOTES & PICTURES

I'VE SEEN IT... Eating ◯   Flying ◯   Nesting ◯

SWALLOW

Difficult to identify because they are rarely seen near the ground, **swallows are extremely agile flyers.** They can be seen swooping through the air as they hunt for insects to eat. Their wings are long and pointed and their tails are deeply forked, unlike swifts and house martins. Swallows migrate to Europe from Africa in spring. Fewer swallows are coming to the UK than previously, but the reason for this is unknown.

SCALE

Dark-blue feathers on back and wings

Tail measures up to 7 cm in length and is deeply forked

Distinctive red throat

Pale cream feathers underneath

Wings are long and pointed

IN THE... Garden ◯ Park ◯ School field ◯

BIRDS

FACT FILE

Scientific name *Columba palumbus*

Size 40–42 cm

Wingspan 75–80 cm

Call Soft cooing

Breeding Two eggs in spring, can breed throughout the year

SUPER FACT

Most birds drink water by gulping it, then throwing their heads back, so the water pours down their throats. Pigeons, however, suck water using their beaks like straws.

PHOTO FILE

Pigeons are sociable birds and often live and feed in large flocks, particularly in towns and villages.

MY NOTES & PICTURES

I'VE SEEN IT... Eating ◯ Flying ◯ Nesting ◯

WOOD PIGEON

The largest of all European pigeons, wood pigeons are commonly seen in gardens, parks woodlands and around farms. Their feathers are mostly grey with a pinkish breast. As they have unusually dense, heavy feathers, they often appear almost round. They can be recognized when they walk by their distinctive waddle. Pigeons feed on a range of foods, and although they often eat seeds, they will eat almost anything on a bird table.

SCALE

Bright-yellow eyes

White and green bars on neck

Grey plumage on upper parts

Plump body

Narrow white bar visible on edge of wing

FACT FILE

Scientific name *Troglodytes troglodytes*

Size 9–10 cm

Wingspan 13–17 cm

Call Loud trills and warbling

Breeding 5–8 white eggs with reddish spots, from April to July

SUPER FACT

Wrens can travel many kilometres in search of food, or to find habitats that are sheltered from harsh weather.

PHOTO FILE

Wrens scurry around looking for small insects and spiders. They pick them out of cracks using their slender beaks.

MY NOTES & PICTURES

I'VE SEEN IT... Eating ◯ Flying ◯ Nesting ◯

WREN

One of the smallest birds that visit gardens, wrens are small, stocky, restless birds. They can be seen rushing around, particularly under trees or bushes where they are well camouflaged. They have brown backs, and brown-and-cream eye stripes. Their pert tails are constantly moving. Wrens use grass and leaves to build their globe-shaped nests in bushes, trees and holes in walls. The nests are lined with feathers.

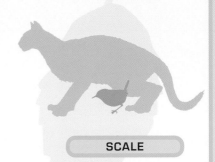

SCALE

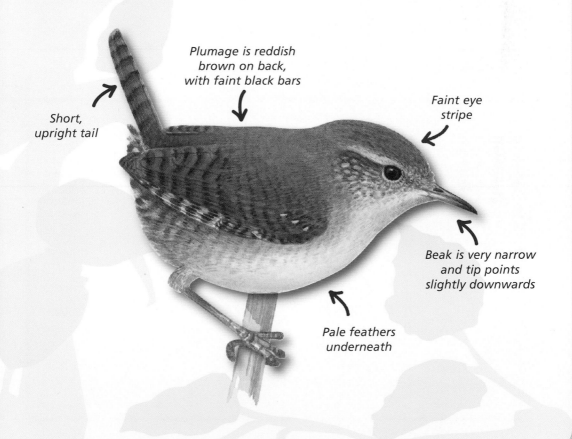

Plumage is reddish brown on back, with faint black bars

Faint eye stripe

Short, upright tail

Beak is very narrow and tip points slightly downwards

Pale feathers underneath

FACT FILE

Scientific name *Meles meles*

Size 67–90 cm

Weight 8–12 kg

Litter size 1–5 cubs

Life expectancy Six years

SUPER FACT

Badgers use their strong claws and powerful legs to dig up bee and wasp nests in order to feed on honey and larvae.

PHOTO FILE

Badgers live in communities, or clans, and hide away in their huge networks of burrows and tunnels called 'setts'.

MY NOTES & PICTURES

I'VE SEEN IT... Juvenile   Adult

BADGER

These animals live in the countryside, in woodland and on large commons. Badgers occasionally wander into gardens and farmland, but as they are nocturnal, seeing a badger is rare. If they come close to human homes, they may be searching for food, and scavenge in rubbish bins. Badgers are omnivorous – they will eat both meat and plants. Male badgers are called boars, the females are called sows, and their young are known as cubs.

SCALE

Short tail (females have bushier tails than males)

Thick, coarse, slate-grey fur

Small, pointed head and short neck

Short, strong legs with sharp claws for digging

Black stripes mark its white face

MAMMALS

FACT FILE

Scientific name *Lepus europaeus*

Size 50–80 cm

Weight 4–7 kg

Litter size Up to 4 leverets

Life expectancy 10–13 years

SUPER FACT

Courtship takes place in spring, giving rise to the phrase 'mad March hare'. Females stand on their hind legs and 'box' one another in a fight over mates!

PHOTO FILE

To avoid being seen by predators, hares keep very still and crouch low. They hold their ears back, listening for any sudden movements.

MY NOTES & PICTURES

I'VE SEEN A... Juvenile ◯ Adult ◯

BROWN HARE

Very fast runners, brown hares can reach speeds of 60 km/h when trying to escape a predator. Brown hares have orangey-brown fur and long slender ears with black tips. Hares are herbivores (they only eat plants). They are hunted by foxes, and young hares may be caught by birds of prey. Hares are often found in open grassland and may wander into nearby gardens, but they are easily scared away.

SCALE

Black-tipped ears

Ears are similar length to head

Orangey-brown fur

White chest fur

Long limbs for quick movement

IN THE... Garden ◯ Park ◯ School field ◯

FACT FILE

Scientific name *Rattus norvegicus*

Size 11–28 cm

Weight 200–400 g

Litter size 6–10 young

Life expectancy 12–18 months

SUPER FACT

Compost heaps are a perfect place for rats to breed. The compost keeps them warm, and there is a steady supply of food.

PHOTO FILE

Brown rats are rarely seen because they are most active at night. They are omnivores and often steal eggs from other animals.

MY NOTES & PICTURES

I'VE SEEN A... Juvenile Adult

COMMON RAT

Also known as brown rats, they live almost everywhere that humans live. They are found in towns, cities and the countryside – anywhere they can find food. They are often associated with dirty places, such as rubbish heaps and sewers, but rats also live in hedgerows and fields. They are highly intelligent creatures with natural curiosity. They can live in large groups, or colonies, and fight one another for the best territory.

SCALE

Brown fur on back

Small eyes (and poor eyesight)

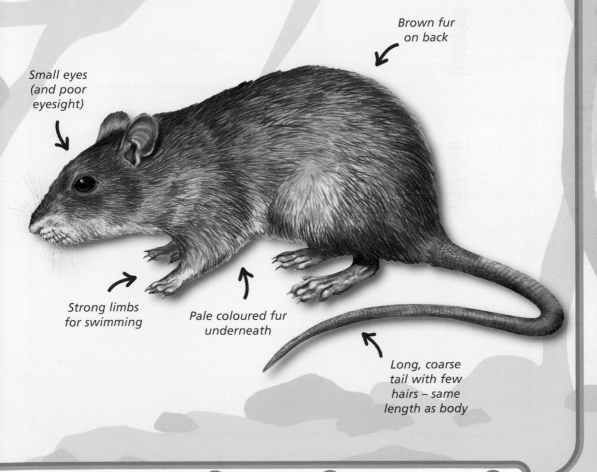

Strong limbs for swimming

Pale coloured fur underneath

Long, coarse tail with few hairs – same length as body

MAMMALS

FACT FILE

Scientific name *Felis catus*

Size 40–60 cm

Weight 2.5–7 kg

Litter size 3–5 kittens

Life expectancy 1–3 years

SUPER FACT

Many small organizations help to care for feral cats by feeding them or providing veterinary care. Few wild cats can become pets as they are too scared of people.

PHOTO FILE

Feral cats have to find their own food. When hunting prey, such as birds and mice, they crouch low, waiting for the moment to pounce.

MY NOTES & PICTURES

I'VE SEEN A... Juvenile ◯ Adult ◯

FERAL CAT

Many feral cats were once unwanted pets. They are not a different type of cat to pet cats – they just have a different lifestyle because they live in the wild. They should also not be confused with wildcats, which are a different species. Feral cats mainly have a tabby pattern, rather than the pure colour of pet cats. They live in farms, parks or gardens, often in large groups.

SCALE

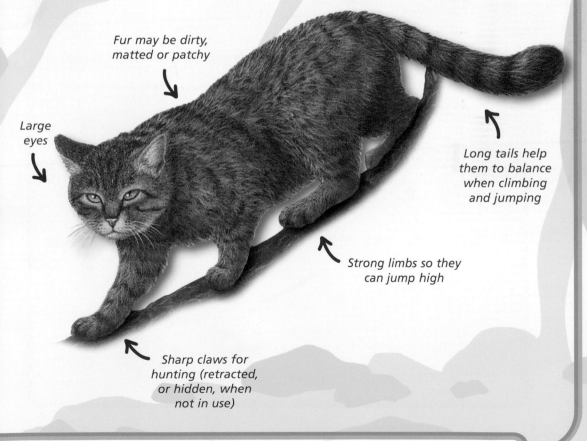

Fur may be dirty, matted or patchy

Large eyes

Long tails help them to balance when climbing and jumping

Strong limbs so they can jump high

Sharp claws for hunting (retracted, or hidden, when not in use)

IN THE... Garden ○ Park ○ School field ○

FACT FILE

Scientific name *Microtus agrestis*

Size 8–13 cm

Weight 15–50 g

Litter size 2–7 young

Life expectancy 1–2 years

SUPER FACT

One female can have up to five litters a year. Each litter contains up to 5 babies. This is a total of 25 babies a year!

PHOTO FILE

Voles are rarely seen as they hide away from predators amongst foliage and leaf litter. They dig burrows to nest in.

MY NOTES & PICTURES

I'VE SEEN A... Juvenile ◯ Adult ◯

FIELD VOLE

Also known as short-tailed voles, field voles are one of Europe's most common mammals, although they are rarely spotted. They mostly live in grassland, scrub, woodland and hedgerows. The diet of field voles is mostly grass, so they live where they can find a plentiful supply and they may come into gardens that border countryside. They have grey-brown fur on their backs, and creamy-white fur underneath.

SCALE

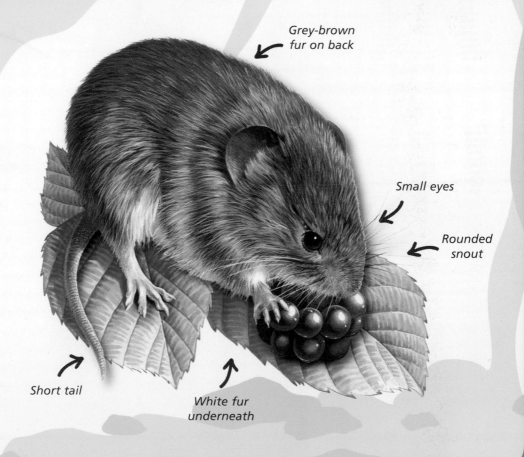

Grey-brown
fur on back

Small eyes

Rounded
snout

Short tail

White fur
underneath

FACT FILE

Scientific name *Sciurus carolinensis*

Size 22–30 cm plus tail

Weight 400–600 g

Litter size 2–5 young

Life expectancy 6–9 years

SUPER FACT

Squirrels build large nests, called dreys, in trees. The outer frame is made from twigs, and the inside is then lined with dry leaves and grass.

PHOTO FILE

Squirrels are great climbers. They strip trees and bird feeders of their nuts, and bury much of their hoard to eat later in the year.

MY NOTES & PICTURES

I'VE SEEN A... Juvenile ◯ Adult ◯

GREY SQUIRREL

Originally from America, grey squirrels are now a common species of mammal, found in parks, gardens and woodland habitats. They have stocky bodies covered in thick, grey fur, and long arching tails. They are active during the day, scurrying about on the ground or in trees, looking for food, such as nuts, shoots and bulbs.

SCALE

Grey fur flecked with rust-coloured hair

Long, bushy tail

No tufts of fur on tips of ears (unlike red squirrels)

Short front limbs with paws

White fur underneath

FACT FILE

Scientific name *Erinaceus europaeus*

Size 20–30 cm

Weight 1–2 kg

Litter size 2–7 young

Life expectancy 3–5 years

SUPER FACT

Young hedgehogs are born blind and helpless. Their mother cares for them for four weeks before they can leave the nest.

PHOTO FILE

When hedgehogs feel threatened, they curl up into a prickly ball, erecting their spines. Few predators are able to unroll and attack them.

MY NOTES & PICTURES

I'VE SEEN A... Juvenile ◯ Adult ◯

HEDGEHOG

These prickly mammals are welcome visitors to the garden, as they eat many pests. Hedgehogs are carnivores and eat slugs, worms, beetles, carrion, eggs and nestlings. They normally live alone and can walk for several kilometres at night as they look for food. These small animals are preyed upon by badgers and foxes. Hedgehogs hibernate from October to April in compost heaps and bonfire piles. They can be injured, or burnt, accidentally by gardeners.

SCALE

Rounded body
covered with
yellow-tipped spines

Pointed
face

Short legs and feet
equipped with sharp
claws for digging

Coarse fur
underneath

IN THE... Garden ◯ Park ◯ School field ◯

MAMMALS

FACT FILE

Scientific name *Mus musculus*

Size 6–10 cm

Weight 12–22 g

Litter size 4–8 young

Life expectancy 1–2 years

SUPER FACT

Wood mice have orangey-brown fur. They sometimes enter houses looking for food. They are good climbers and can often be spotted in trees.

PHOTO FILE

Mice are small rodents and are able to fit into the smallest of spaces to search for food, such as seeds, berries, snails and spiders.

MY NOTES & PICTURES

I'VE SEEN A... Juvenile Adult ◯

HOUSE MOUSE

Although mice are very common mammals, it is unusual to see them because they are most active at night. House mice first came from Asia, but they are now found around the world, almost anywhere that humans live. During winter they may come into houses, often setting up home in roof spaces, under floorboards or in outbuildings.

SCALE

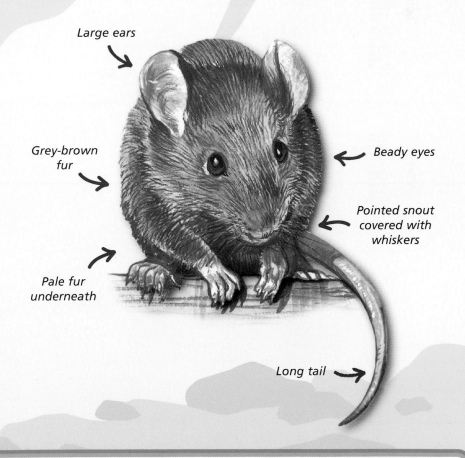

Large ears

Grey-brown fur

Pale fur underneath

Beady eyes

Pointed snout covered with whiskers

Long tail

MAMMALS

FACT FILE

Scientific name *Talpa europaea*

Size 11–16 cm

Weight 70–130 g

Litter size 3–4 young

Life expectancy 2–3 years

SUPER FACT

Moles are well-known for their digging skills. They use their shovel-like forelimbs to scoop earth away to create a tunnel.

PHOTO FILE

Moles live underground. When they dig their way to the surface, they create mounds of earth called molehills.

MY NOTES & PICTURES

I'VE SEEN A... Juvenile Adult

MOLE

It is unusual to see moles as they spend most of their lives **underground, digging or sleeping.** They have soft, dense, grey-black fur, pink noses, whiskers, and very small eyes. They eat earthworms and insect grubs, which they find using their excellent senses of smell and hearing. They store hundreds of worms in underground larders so they have a ready supply of food.

SCALE

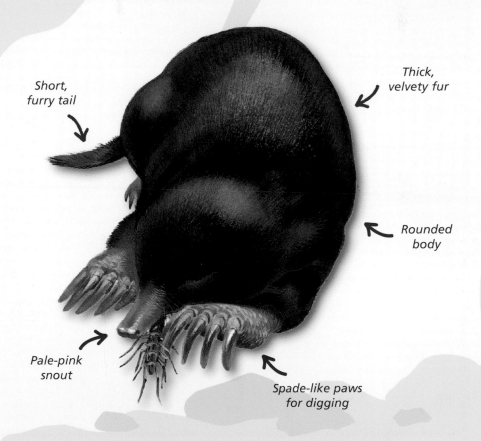

Short, furry tail

Thick, velvety fur

Rounded body

Pale-pink snout

Spade-like paws for digging

MAMMALS

FACT FILE

Scientific name *Pipistrellus pipistrellus*

Size 3–5 cm (body)

Weight 3–10 g

Litter size 1–2 young

Life expectancy 4–10 years

SUPER FACT

To catch prey, bats send out noises, and can tell by the echoes that bounce back whether insects are close. The echoes also help them to judge the size of the prey.

PHOTO FILE

Bats are the only mammals that can fly. In the evening, pipistrelles are the first bats to appear as they hunt for insects.

MY NOTES & PICTURES

I'VE SEEN A... Juvenile ○ Adult ○

PIPISTRELLE BAT

Pipistrelles are the smallest and most common bats in the UK. They are unlikely to be spotted in winter, but during summer they swoop and dive, with a characteristic jerky flight, over gardens. They roost in buildings, and can squeeze through tiny gaps to find somewhere sheltered and dry to rest. They feed on flying insects, and one bat can eat more than 3000 insects in one night.

SCALE

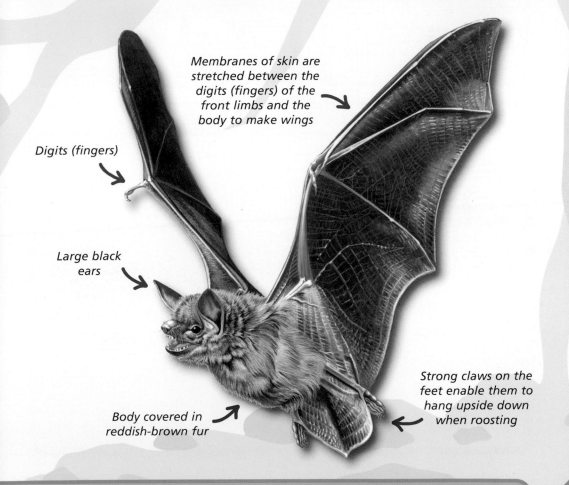

Membranes of skin are stretched between the digits (fingers) of the front limbs and the body to make wings

Digits (fingers)

Large black ears

Strong claws on the feet enable them to hang upside down when roosting

Body covered in reddish-brown fur

MAMMALS

FACT FILE

Scientific name *Sorex minutus*

Size 4–6 cm

Weight 4–6 g

Litter size 4–7 young

Life expectancy 3–12 months

SUPER FACT

Pygmy shrews rarely live for more than one year. They may not survive harsh winters, and they are preyed upon by large mammals, such as cats, foxes and stoats.

PHOTO FILE

Pygmy shrews have to eat every few hours to provide their bodies with energy, or they may die. They feed on insects, worms and carrion.

MY NOTES & PICTURES

I'VE SEEN A... Juvenile   Adult

PYGMY SHREW

These small rodent-like mammals are often found near compost heaps in the garden. Pygmy shrews run away quickly when disturbed, making it difficult to identify them for sure – at first glance, they look like young mice or rats. Pygmy shrews are common visitors to gardens and they are the UK's smallest mammal.

SCALE

Brown fur on back

Long snout covered with whiskers

Short legs

Grey-white fur underneath

Long, thick tail, measuring up to 4 cm

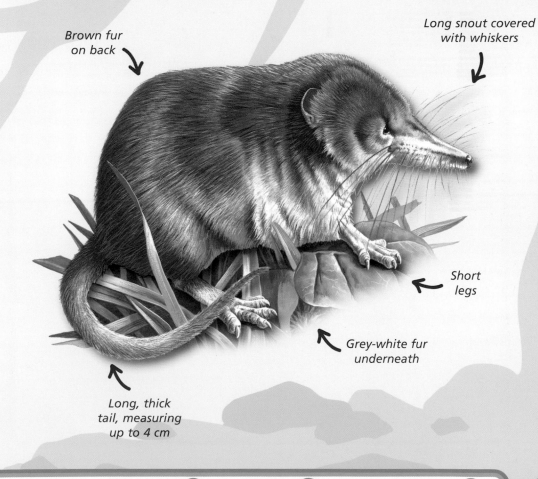

MAMMALS

FACT FILE

Scientific name *Vulpes vulpes*
Size 50–80 cm
Weight 2–7 kg
Litter size 4–5 cubs
Life expectancy 2–4 years

SUPER FACT

Foxes are secretive animals, except during breeding season in winter, when they become very noisy.

PHOTO FILE

Cubs are born completely blind in early spring. When they are a few months old, they can often be seen playing in gardens.

MY NOTES & PICTURES

I'VE SEEN A...   Juvenile ◯   Adult ◯

RED FOX

Once mainly found in the countryside, red foxes are now widespread in towns and cities – where they have discovered a new source of food. They often scavenge from rubbish bins and will eat almost any food they find lying around. Females are called vixens and are smaller than males, which are called dogs. Foxes are most active at night, especially at dawn and dusk.

SCALE

Reddish-brown fur (may be mangy, dirty or patchy)

Black fur on ears

Long, thick tail, known as a 'brush'

White chest and throat

Black fur on legs

IN THE... Garden ◯ Park ◯ School field ◯

MAMMALS

FACT FILE

Scientific name *Mustela erminea*

Size 23–30 cm

Weight 1–4 kg

Litter size 6–12 kits

Life expectancy 2–5 years

SUPER FACT

In winter, stoats were once hunted for their ermine pelts (fur), which were used for stoles and robes worn by royalty and judges. Nowadays, artificial fur is used.

PHOTO FILE

Stoats are carnivores. They hunt both day and night and their prey includes voles, mice, birds, rabbits and hares.

MY NOTES & PICTURES

I'VE SEEN A... Juvenile Adult

STOAT

These mammals are closely related to **weasels, pine martens, otters, minks and badgers.** However, stoats are larger than weasels and have reddish-brown fur. In northern parts of the UK, their fur turns white in winter. They can climb trees, swim and jump. Stoats use their excellent sense of smell to find their prey, which they kill with a single bite to the back of the neck. Thanks to their long and slender bodies, stoats can chase their prey into burrows.

SCALE

Small eyes and ears

Reddish-brown fur on back

White fur underneath

Black-tipped tail

Long, slender body

IN THE... Garden Park School field

MAMMALS

FACT FILE

Scientific name *Mustela nivalis*

Size 15–25 cm

Weight 50–100 g

Litter size 3–8 young

Life expectancy 1–2 years

SUPER FACT

Weasels sometimes leap around strangely. It was thought they did this to confuse their prey, but it actually may be due to a worm that lives in weasels' noses.

PHOTO FILE

In northern Europe, the weasel's fur turns white to provide camouflage in the snow. It is then known as the weasel form of ermine.

MY NOTES & PICTURES

I'VE SEEN A... Juvenile   Adult

WEASEL

Found in woods, farms and large gardens, weasels are active both at night and during the day. They sleep in burrows that have been abandoned by badgers or rabbits. Weasels live alone and mark their territory with strong scent. They are busy mammals and need to eat regularly to maintain their energy levels – they cannot survive more than 24 hours without food.

SCALE

Small, flattened head

Long, slender body

Brown fur on back

White fur underneath

Short legs

BUGS

FACT FILE

Scientific name *Formicidae* family

Habitat Underground, compost heaps

Size 4–5 mm

Wings Males and queen ants

Breeding Queens lay thousands of eggs every month

SUPER FACT

Colonies in tropical regions can contain millions of ants. Some, such as driver and army ants, eat almost anything and can even strip a tethered horse to its skeleton.

PHOTO FILE

Ants help plants to grow by breaking up the soil, and by carrying seeds and other food around the garden.

MY NOTES & PICTURES

I'VE SEEN IT... Feeding ◯   Flying ◯

ANT

Found in almost every habitat on land in the world, ants live in large colonies. They can be seen busily scurrying around a garden from spring to autumn, but are seen less often in winter when the temperatures are low. A colony of ants is divided into different types – the queen ant, female workers, and male ants. Some defend the nest, for example, while others are involved in reproduction.

ACTUAL SIZE

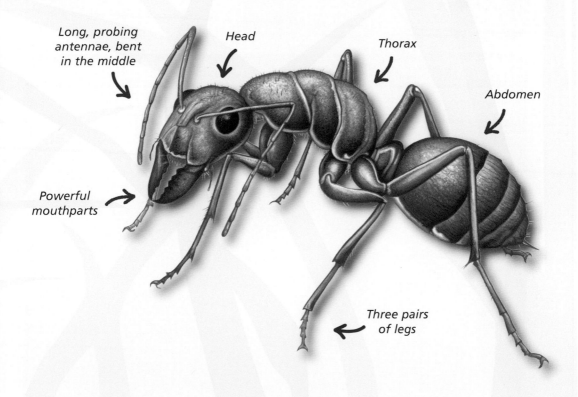

Long, probing antennae, bent in the middle

Head

Thorax

Abdomen

Powerful mouthparts

Three pairs of legs

BUGS

FACT FILE

Scientific name *Aphidae* family

Habitat Tender plant stems, leaves and buds

Size 3–5 mm

Wings Two pairs or none

Breeding Seasonal

SUPER FACT

Aphids produce a sticky substance, called honeydew, which ants collect from them for food. In return, the ants protect the aphids from other predators.

PHOTO FILE

Groups of aphids can often be seen clustered around a stem or bud as they feed on the plant sap.

MY NOTES & PICTURES

I'VE SEEN IT... Feeding ◯   Flying ◯

APHID

There are about 4000 types of aphid, and many of those are garden pests. The most well-known aphid is the common greenfly, which lives on plants. Aphids use their long, slender mouthparts to pierce a hole in the stems of plants. Then they eat the liquid food that pours out of the hole. Aphids also damage plants by passing viruses between them. Ladybirds and lacewings are important predators of aphids.

ACTUAL SIZE

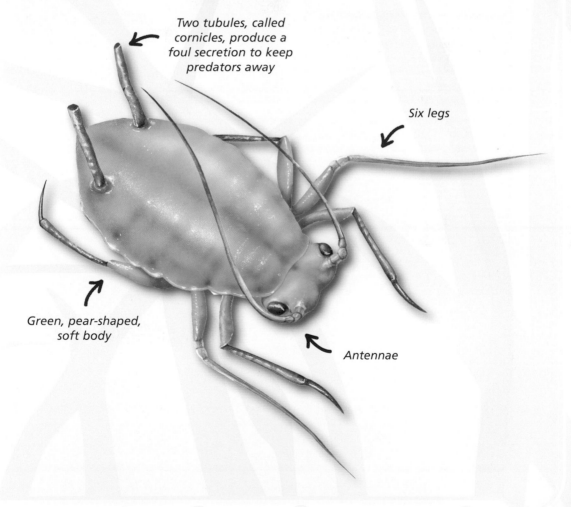

Two tubules, called cornicles, produce a foul secretion to keep predators away

Six legs

Green, pear-shaped, soft body

Antennae

BUGS

FACT FILE

Scientific name *Apidae* family

Habitat Gardens, woodlands, parks

Size 10–30 mm

Wings Two pairs

Breeding Queens lay more than 100 eggs a day

SUPER FACT

Bees communicate with each other in lots of different ways, including 'dancing'. Honey bees returning to the hive use a dance to tell other bees where to find nectar.

PHOTO FILE

Honey bees collect nectar from flowers, which they use to produce honey in their hives. They may visit up to 1000 flowers in one day.

MY NOTES & PICTURES

I'VE SEEN IT... Feeding ◯   Flying ◯

BEE

One of most important groups of insect, bees benefit both gardeners and farmers. They pollinate many plants, which is an essential part of fruit and seed production. Garden bumble bees, like honey bees, collect nectar from plants, and feed pollen to their young. They are not aggressive insects, and rarely sting. However, unlike honey bees, bumble bees can sting more than once. Some types of bumble bee are in danger of becoming extinct.

ACTUAL SIZE

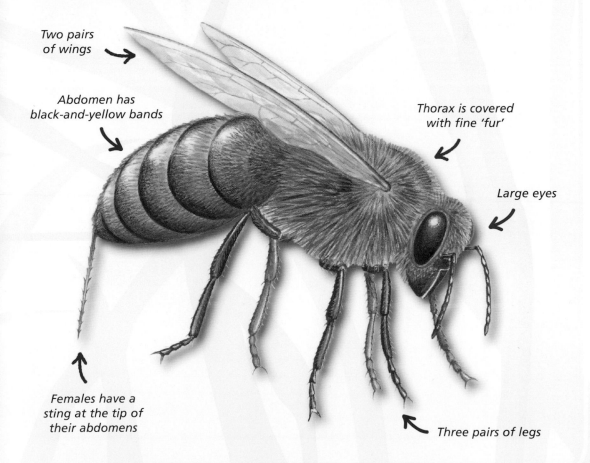

Two pairs of wings

Abdomen has black-and-yellow bands

Thorax is covered with fine 'fur'

Large eyes

Females have a sting at the tip of their abdomens

Three pairs of legs

FACT FILE

Scientific name *Calliphora vomitoria*

Habitat Gardens and houses

Size 12–15 mm

Wings One pair

Breeding Larvae are called maggots

SUPER FACT

Blowflies eat the flesh of living animals. They lay their eggs in open wounds. The maggots hatch within eight hours, then eat the unhealthy flesh.

PHOTO FILE

Uncovered food, dog faeces and rubbish are favourite places for these flies to settle and feed, and spread disease.

MY NOTES & PICTURES

I'VE SEEN IT...   Feeding   Flying

BLUEBOTTLE

Easily recognized by the shiny metallic sheen to their bodies, bluebottles belong to a group of insects called blowflies. They visit gardens where there is rubbish, food or animal faeces, and they are unwelcome visitors since they spread diseases. When the eggs hatch, small, white carrot-shaped maggots emerge to feed and grow. The maggots dig into the ground and pupate, emerging as adult flies about ten days later.

ACTUAL SIZE

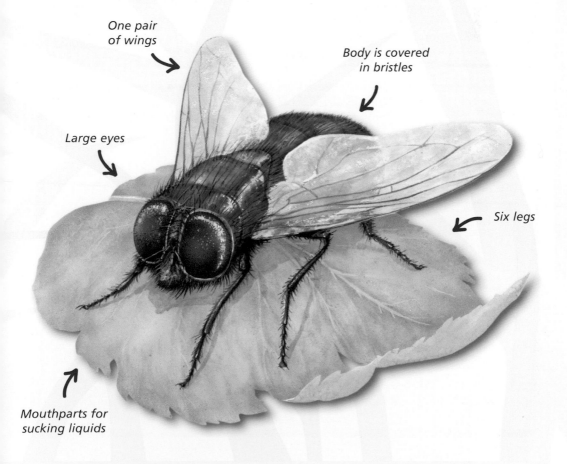

One pair of wings

Body is covered in bristles

Large eyes

Six legs

Mouthparts for sucking liquids

IN THE... Garden ◯ Park ◯ School field ◯

BUGS

FACT FILE

Scientific name *Caribidae* family

Habitat Woodlands and gardens

Size Various

Wings Two pairs

Breeding Larvae are called grubs

SUPER FACT

The chemicals needed to produce this beetle's boiling fluid are stored in the abdomen. They mix together in a special chamber just before being sprayed at a predator.

PHOTO FILE

There are more than 500 types of bombardier beetle. They live in woodlands and grasslands and are usually small and dull in colour.

MY NOTES & PICTURES

I'VE SEEN IT... Feeding ◯   Flying ◯

BOMBARDIER BEETLE

Like all ground beetles, bombardier beetles lay their eggs where the newly hatched grubs will find food, such as in a pile of rotting leaves. The grubs grow quickly and moult, or shed, their skin as they get bigger. Eventually they pupate, and during this time of change the grub grows into an adult beetle. Bombardier beetles cannot fly. To defend themselves from predators, they spray a burning liquid from their rear ends.

ACTUAL SIZE

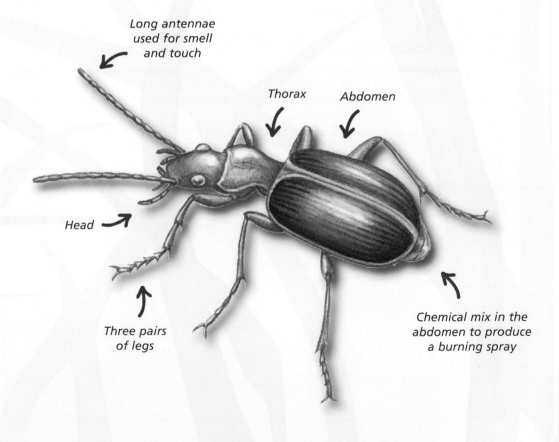

Long antennae used for smell and touch

Thorax

Abdomen

Head

Three pairs of legs

Chemical mix in the abdomen to produce a burning spray

IN THE... Garden ◯　　　Park ◯　　　School field ◯

BUGS

FACT FILE

Scientific name *Pieris rapae*

Habitat Gardens and fields

Size 45 mm wingspan

Wings Two pairs

Breeding Larvae are called caterpillars

SUPER FACT

Adult butterflies emerge from their pupae in July. They breed twice in summer and the last generation spends winter, protected from cold, as a pupa or chrysalis.

PHOTO FILE

The larvae, or caterpillars, of the cabbage white butterfly are green with black stripes on their backs and sides.

MY NOTES & PICTURES

I'VE SEEN IT...   Feeding   Flying

CABBAGE WHITE BUTTERFLY

These are small white, cream or pale-yellow butterflies. Females have two black spots on each of their forewings, and males have just one. They live in gardens, meadows and fields. Adults suck nectar from flowers, such as dandelions, and the larvae eat leaves of plants from the mustard family, such as cabbage, broccoli and cauliflower. Adults can often be seen in mating rituals, flying upwards in spirals.

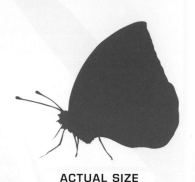

ACTUAL SIZE

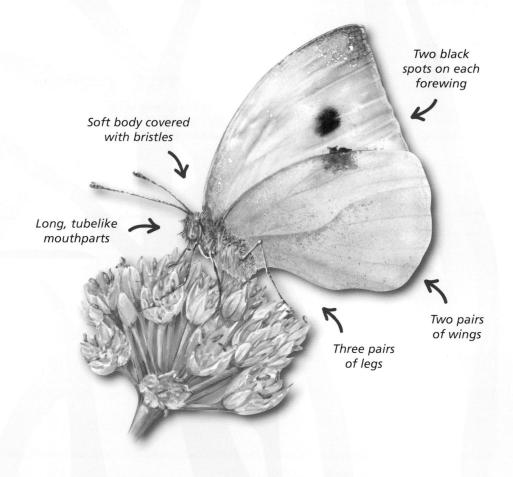

Two black spots on each forewing

Soft body covered with bristles

Long, tubelike mouthparts

Three pairs of legs

Two pairs of wings

IN THE... Garden   Park   School field

BUGS

FACT FILE

Scientific name
Centipede *Chilopoda* superclass
Millipede *Diplopoda* superclass

Habitat Leaf litter and soil

Size 7–40 mm

Breeding Larvae moult and grow many times

SUPER FACT

The world's largest centipedes, scolopendrids, live in South America. They measure up to 30 cm in length and use their venomous claws to catch mice and frogs.

PHOTO FILE

Snake millipedes have shiny, cylinder-shaped bodies. They live in leaf litter and climb trees and fences to feed at night.

MY NOTES & PICTURES

I'VE SEEN IT... Feeding ◯ Flying ◯

CENTIPEDE & MILLIPEDE

These bugs aren't actually insects, but belong to a group of creatures called myriapods. Centipedes and millipedes have long bodies that are divided into many segments. Centipedes have one pair of legs on each segment, while millipedes have two. The number of segments varies. The common centipede is chestnut brown in colour and adults have 15 pairs of legs. They hunt for insects, slugs and worms at night. Flat-backed millipedes live in compost heaps and leaf litter, and eat plant matter.

ACTUAL SIZE

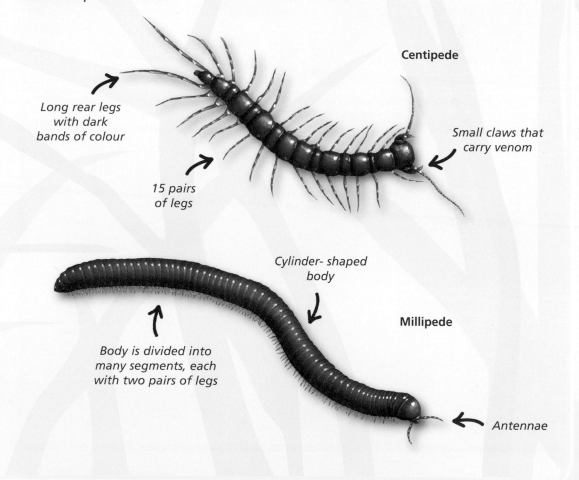

Centipede

Long rear legs with dark bands of colour

Small claws that carry venom

15 pairs of legs

Cylinder- shaped body

Millipede

Body is divided into many segments, each with two pairs of legs

Antennae

IN THE... Garden ◯ Park ◯ School field ◯

BUGS

FACT FILE

Scientific name *Cydia pomonella*

Habitat Where apple trees grow

Size 10–20 mm wingspan

Wings Two pairs

Breeding Larvae are called caterpillars

SUPER FACT

The large eye-shaped markings on the tips of the codling moth's forewings distract and confuse predators, such as birds.

PHOTO FILE

Codling moth larvae are also known as apple maggots because they mainly feed on apples. They have white bodies and brown heads.

MY NOTES & PICTURES

I'VE SEEN IT... Feeding ◯   Flying ◯

CODLING MOTH

The larvae of the codling moth are pests that eat the fruit of some trees, particularly apple and pear. Adult females lay a single egg on a leaf of the tree. When the larva emerges, it bores into apples or pears, making long tunnels as it eats its way through the fruit flesh. The larva pupates under bark or in leaf litter, emerging as an adult between November and February, depending on the conditions.

ACTUAL SIZE

Copper-coloured bands

Grey-and-brown mottled wings

Grey body and head

One pair of antennae

Large eyes made up of many small lenses

Three pairs of legs

IN THE... Garden ⦾ Park ⦾ School field ⦾

BUGS

FACT FILE

Scientific name *Polygonia c-album*

Habitat Gardens and meadows

Size 40–55 mm wingspan

Wings Two pairs

Breeding Larvae are called caterpillars

SUPER FACT

The caterpillar of the comma butterfly is black with red and white markings, giving it the appearance of a bird dropping. It is covered in spines.

PHOTO FILE

The underside of a comma's hind wing has a white comma-shaped mark. Like many butterflies, they emerge from their pupae in spring.

MY NOTES & PICTURES

I'VE SEEN IT... Feeding   Flying

COMMA BUTTERFLY

With dull patterns on the underside of their wings, commas can be difficult to see among dead leaves. This camouflage helps to protect the butterflies from predators, such as birds and bats, when they overwinter and hang from leaves. Commas live in gardens, hedges and woodlands where they can find flowers that will supply them with nectar as adults, and leaves, such as stinging nettles, as larvae.

ACTUAL SIZE

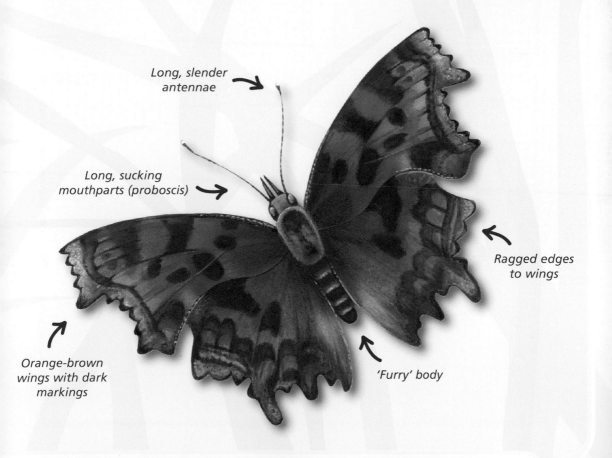

Long, slender antennae

Long, sucking mouthparts (proboscis)

Ragged edges to wings

Orange-brown wings with dark markings

'Furry' body

IN THE... Garden ◯ Park ◯ School field

BUGS

FACT FILE

Scientific name *Tipula paludosa*

Habitat Grasslands and gardens

Size 30–60 mm

Wings One pair

Breeding Larvae are called leatherjackets

SUPER FACT

Crane flies are slow and easy to catch. They have small balancing limbs, called halteres, on either side of their bodies, which help to keep them stable when they fly.

PHOTO FILE

Adult crane flies have short lives. They are preyed upon by birds, particularly robins and starlings, but can shed their legs if caught.

MY NOTES & PICTURES

I'VE SEEN IT... Feeding   Flying

CRANE FLY

Crane flies are more commonly known as **daddy-long-legs.** They have long, slender bodies and unusually long legs. In tropical regions, their legs can measure up to 10 cm, but 3–6 cm is normal in cooler places. Adults are usually seen in the garden in autumn, especially during periods of damp or foggy weather. The larva of the crane fly is called a leatherjacket due to its tough, leathery skin. They live in soil where they feed on roots.

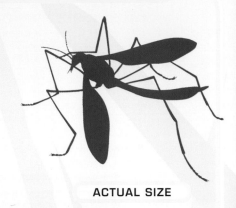

ACTUAL SIZE

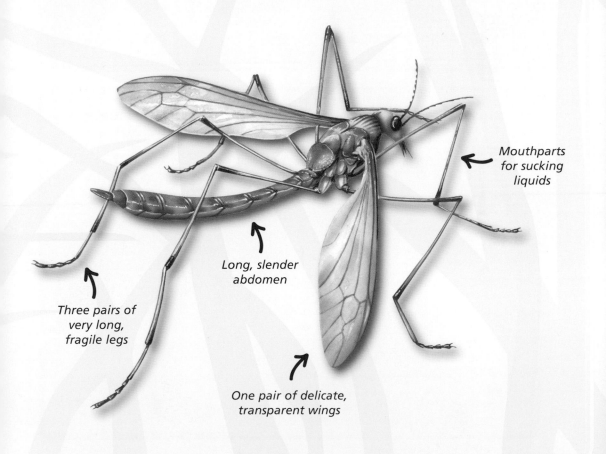

Mouthparts for sucking liquids

Long, slender abdomen

Three pairs of very long, fragile legs

One pair of delicate, transparent wings

BUGS

FACT FILE

Scientific name *Odonata* order

Habitat Near slow-moving or still water

Size 2–9 cm

Wings Two pairs

Breeding Larvae are called nymphs

SUPER FACT

In ancient times, dragonflies and damselflies were much bigger than today. Fossils of dragonflies show that their wingspans reached up to 75 cm!

PHOTO FILE

When they are at rest, damselflies usually hold their wings together above their bodies. They can see in almost every direction.

MY NOTES & PICTURES

I'VE SEEN IT... Feeding ◯   Flying ◯

DRAGONFLY

Dragonflies and damselflies are superb flyers and dart around in summer and autumn, visiting woodlands and gardens where there is water. They can be easily recognized by their long, slender bodies with colourful bands. Dragonflies have huge eyes that almost meet and give them great vision. Both dragonflies and damselflies spend most of their early lives underwater in ponds or lakes, as nymphs. They can breathe underwater using their gills.

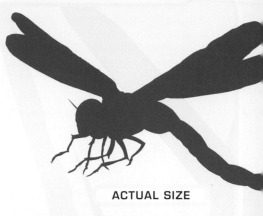

ACTUAL SIZE

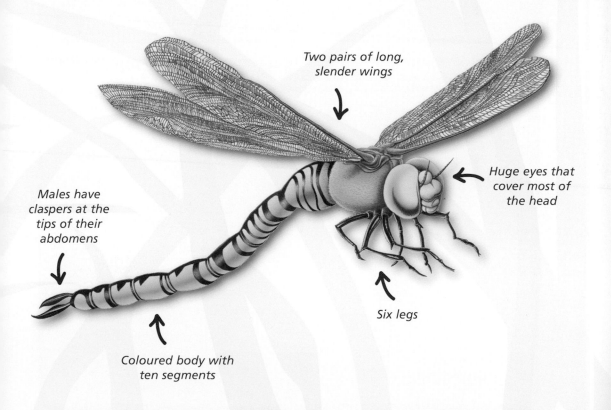

Two pairs of long, slender wings

Huge eyes that cover most of the head

Males have claspers at the tips of their abdomens

Six legs

Coloured body with ten segments

IN THE... Garden ◯ Park ◯ School field

BUGS

FACT FILE

Scientific name *Lumbricus terrestris*

Habitat Underground, compost heaps

Size 9–30 cm

Breeding Young are small, but fully-formed worms

SUPER FACT

Earthworms are unusual because they have both male and female reproductive organs. They do not fertilize themselves, however, and still come together to mate.

PHOTO FILE

When worms burrow through soil, they leave tell-tale casts, which are mounds of soil that have passed through the worm's body.

MY NOTES & PICTURES

I'VE SEEN IT... Feeding ◯   Flying ◯

EARTHWORM

Earthworms are animals with soft bodies that are divided into many segments. They do not have legs and move by rhythmically contracting and relaxing their muscles. They also have little bristles, called setae, which help them to move through burrows of soil. Earthworms spend most of their time underground, where it is moist. They swallow soil and eat decaying plant matter. Earthworms are good for gardens as they improve soil by bringing air into it.

ACTUAL SIZE

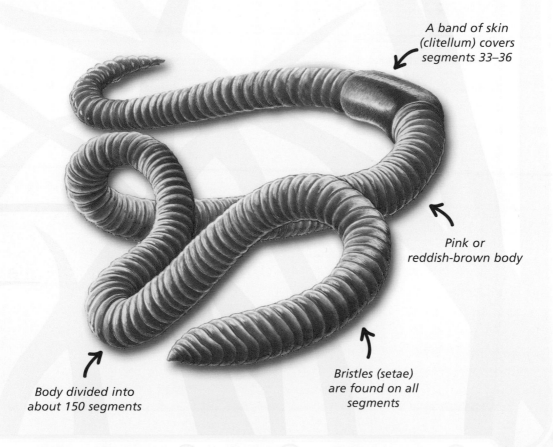

A band of skin (clitellum) covers segments 33–36

Pink or reddish-brown body

Body divided into about 150 segments

Bristles (setae) are found on all segments

BUGS

FACT FILE

Scientific name *Forficula auricularia*

Habitat In soil and under stones

Size 10–15 mm

Wings Two pairs

Breeding Young earwigs appear white when they moult

SUPER FACT

It was once believed that earwigs climbed into people's ears and burrowed into the brain. Mashed earwigs were used in Roman times to treat earache.

PHOTO FILE

Earwigs care for their eggs and young, and will protect them if the nest is disturbed or attacked. It is unusual for insects to do this.

MY NOTES & PICTURES

I'VE SEEN IT... Feeding ◯   Flying ◯

EARWIG

Plentiful in most gardens, earwigs are often found lurking in cracks and crevices where it is dark, and they are hidden from predators. They have long, thin bodies and two pairs of wings – the first of which are leathery and short. Earwigs have pincers, called cerci, on the ends of their abdomen. Cerci are used to help fold the wings back after flight.

ACTUAL SIZE

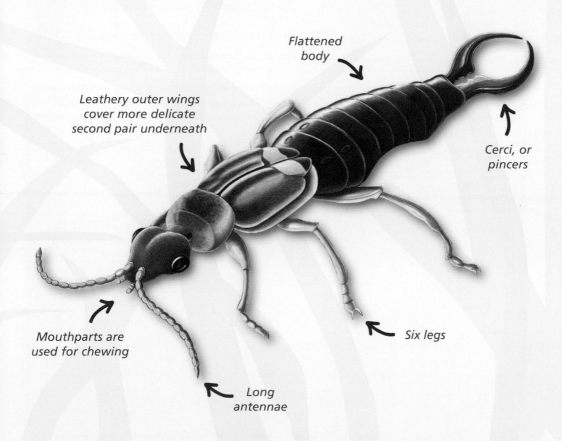

Flattened body

Leathery outer wings cover more delicate second pair underneath

Cerci, or pincers

Mouthparts are used for chewing

Six legs

Long antennae

FACT FILE

Scientific name *Araneus diadematus*

Habitat Gardens, parks and woodlands

Size 10–14 mm (female)

Breeding Young are small, but fully-formed spiders

SUPER FACT

Spiders usually have eight eyes, eight legs, and are venomous. Their bodies are divided into two main segments – the cephalothorax and the abdomen.

PHOTO FILE

Garden spiders use silk to build their webs and capture their prey, such as flies. The fly will become wrapped in silk and then eaten.

MY NOTES & PICTURES

I'VE SEEN IT... Feeding ◯   Flying ◯

GARDEN SPIDER

These spiders are usually brown, beige and black in colour, although patterns do vary. There are mottled white patches on the abdomen, which often look like a cross. Females are about twice the size of males. Garden spiders are common in meadows, farms, woodlands and gardens. They spin silk, which they use to build their webs and to make cocoons to protect their eggs.

ACTUAL SIZE

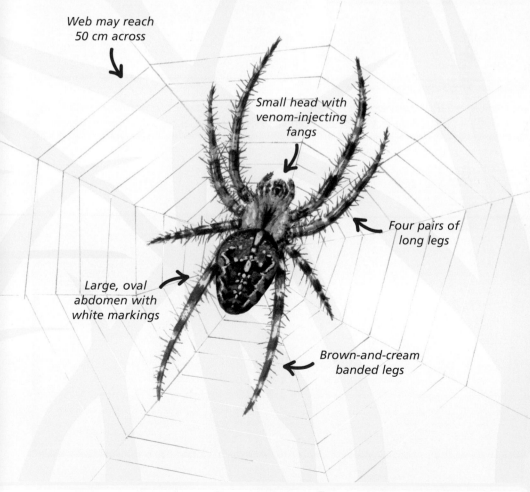

Web may reach 50 cm across

Small head with venom-injecting fangs

Four pairs of long legs

Large, oval abdomen with white markings

Brown-and-cream banded legs

IN THE... Garden ◯ Park ◯ School field ◯

BUGS

FACT FILE

Scientific name *Orthoptera* order

Habitat Grasslands, gardens and woodlands

Size 20–25 mm (female)

Wings Two pairs

Breeding Larvae are called nymphs

SUPER FACT

In some parts of the world grasshoppers are a popular food. Their legs and wings are removed before the body is fried in oil.

PHOTO FILE

Grasshoppers have large eyes and short antennae. Their mouthparts are adapted for eating grass and other tough plant materials.

MY NOTES & PICTURES

I'VE SEEN IT... Feeding ◯   Flying ◯

GRASSHOPPER

With their large wings, grasshoppers and crickets are good flyers, but usually prefer to escape from danger by leaping. Usually green, they are well camouflaged against foliage. They have long, powerful legs that they use for jumping more than 20 times their own body length. Crickets have longer antennae than grasshoppers and can often be heard 'singing' on a summer's evening. The song sounds like a series of loud 'chirrups'.

ACTUAL SIZE

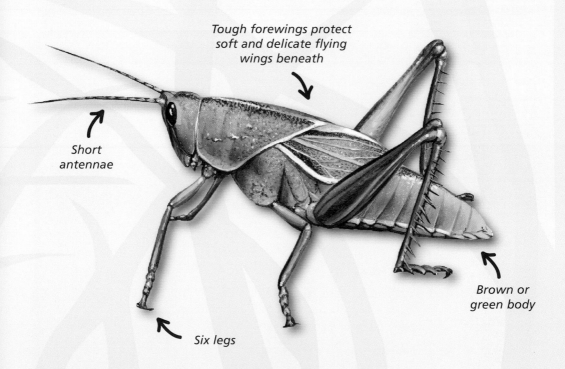

Tough forewings protect soft and delicate flying wings beneath

Short antennae

Brown or green body

Six legs

IN THE... Garden ◯ Park ◯ School field ◯

BUGS

FACT FILE

Scientific name *Palomena prasina*

Habitat Shrubs in gardens, woods and parks

Size 10 mm

Wings Two pairs

Breeding Larvae are called nymphs

SUPER FACT

Shield bugs may look like beetles, but actually they belong to a different group of insects, called bugs, or hemipterans.

PHOTO FILE

Shield bugs were named after their body shape because they look like shields, especially in autumn when they turn bronze in colour.

MY NOTES & PICTURES

I'VE SEEN... Feeding ◯   Flying ◯

GREEN SHIELD BUG

Often found resting on leaves in the sun, green shield bugs are broad and flat in shape. They have hard forewings that protect the second pair of wings. Their sucking mouthparts are used to drink sap from plants. The larvae are similar in shape to adults, but they are black and green. Adults spend winter hibernating in leaf litter and in spring, females lay up to 400 eggs on plants.

ACTUAL SIZE

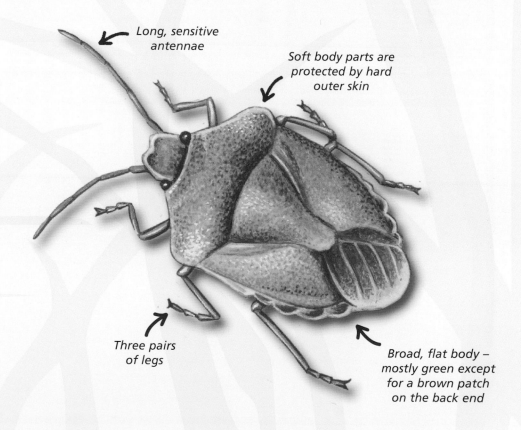

Long, sensitive antennae

Soft body parts are protected by hard outer skin

Three pairs of legs

Broad, flat body – mostly green except for a brown patch on the back end

IN THE... Garden ◯ Park ◯ School field ◯

BUGS

FACT FILE

Scientific name *Phalangium opilio*

Habitat Thick vegetation

Size Up to 10 cm including legs

Wings None

Breeding Young are small, but fully formed

SUPER FACT

Harvestmen do not have spinnerets for secreting silk thread to make nests and webs. They also lack venom glands and do not have a poisonous bite.

PHOTO FILE

Harvestmen catch their prey using their hooked claws. They are able to lose a leg and escape if they are caught by a predator.

MY NOTES & PICTURES

I'VE SEEN... Feeding ◯ Flying ◯

HARVESTMAN

With eight legs, harvestmen belong to the same group of animals as spiders and scorpions – the arachnids. Unlike spiders, their bodies are rounded, without a waist. Females are usually bigger than males, and can lay 20–100 eggs at a time. Their long, skinny legs end in tiny claws and their small mouthparts can produce foul substances to keep predators away. They feed at night, mostly on small invertebrates (animals without backbones).

ACTUAL SIZE

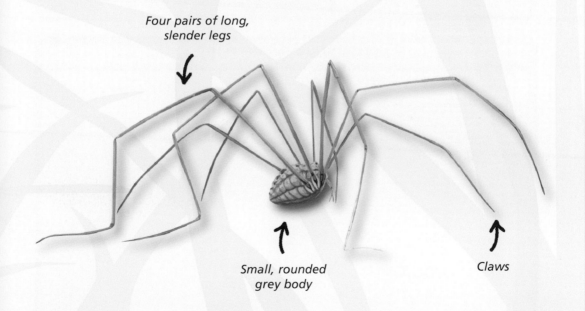

Four pairs of long, slender legs

Small, rounded grey body

Claws

BUGS

FACT FILE

Scientific name *Syrphus ribesii*

Habitat Gardens, parks and woodlands

Size 8–10 mm

Wings One pair

Breeding Green or yellow sluglike larvae

SUPER FACT

Hoverfly larvae emerge from small, white, oval eggs. They are blind and limbless, and have enormous appetites. Several generations hatch in one year.

PHOTO FILE

Hoverflies can be mistaken for wasps because they both have black-and-yellow banding and are similar in size. Hoverflies cannot sting.

MY NOTES & PICTURES

I'VE SEEN... Feeding   Flying

HOVERFLY

Skilled flyers, hoverflies only have one pair of wings, and are often seen darting about and changing direction with speed. Adults are often seen near flowering plants, making a high-pitched buzzing sound as they forage for nectar and pollen. They can hover in one place, with their wings beating so fast that the movement cannot be seen by the human eye.

ACTUAL SIZE

One pair of wings (wasps have two pairs)

Black-and-yellow bands on abdomen

Large eyes made up of many small lenses

Mouthparts are used to feed on pollen and nectar

IN THE... Garden ◯ Park ◯ School field ◯

BUGS

FACT FILE

Scientific name *Coccinella 7-punctata*

Habitat Gardens and woodlands

Size 5–8 mm

Wings Two pairs

Breeding Blue larvae with cream spots

SUPER FACT

When handled, ladybirds produce drops of smelly yellow fluid from their legs to deter predators from eating them. Their bright colours warn predators to stay away.

PHOTO FILE

The seven-spot ladybird has three spots on each elytron. The seventh spot is where the elytra, which protect the soft wings beneath, meet.

MY NOTES & PICTURES

I'VE SEEN... Feeding ◯   Flying ◯

LADYBIRD

Brightly coloured beetles, ladybirds have round bodies and hard wing cases, called elytra. Adults spend winter in large groups, hidden under loose bark on trees or crammed into crevices. Ladybird larvae hatch from small eggs that are glued to plants either singly or in small groups. They mostly eat other soft-bodied animals. Adult ladybirds are important predators of aphids, making them especially welcome in gardens. Thirteen-spot and five-spot ladybirds are very rare and seldom seen in the UK. The two-spot ladybird is smaller than its seven-spotted cousin and their colours vary from region to region.

ACTUAL SIZE

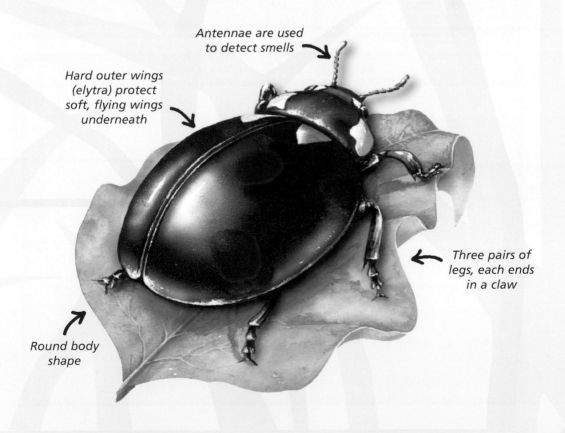

Antennae are used to detect smells

Hard outer wings (elytra) protect soft, flying wings underneath

Three pairs of legs, each ends in a claw

Round body shape

IN THE... Garden ◯   Park ◯   School field ◯

BUGS

FACT FILE

Scientific name *Abraxas grossulariata*

Habitat Meadows and woods

Size 40–50 mm wingspan

Wings Two pairs

Breeding Larvae are called caterpillars

SUPER FACT

Moths and butterflies belong to the same family of insects. Moths usually have drab colours, are active at night and have thick or feathery antennae.

PHOTO FILE

Butterfly and moth wings are covered in thousands of tiny scales. Bright colours are caused by light reflecting off them.

MY NOTES & PICTURES

I'VE SEEN... Feeding ⬤ Flying ⬤

MAGPIE MOTH

Boldly patterned, magpie moths have black-and-white wings with yellow bands. This colouring warns predators, such as birds and spiders, that they taste foul. The adults emerge from their pupae in June and drink nectar from flowers. They can be seen in the garden until August and, unlike many other moths, they are active during the day.

ACTUAL SIZE

Long antennae are used to touch and smell

Three pairs of legs

Orange band crosses the forewings

Forewings are white with black bands and spots

BUGS

FACT FILE

Scientific name *Aedes detritus*

Habitat Near slow-moving or still water

Size 5–8 mm

Wings One pair

Breeding Larvae live in water

SUPER FACT

In hot regions of the world, mosquitoes spread deadly diseases, such as malaria and dengue fever, to people. Only female Anopheles mosquitos spread malaria.

PHOTO FILE

Female mosquitoes suck human blood and, up to one week later, lay their eggs. Eggs can survive for years before hatching.

MY NOTES & PICTURES

I'VE SEEN... Feeding ◯   Flying ◯

MOSQUITO

In spring, adults emerge from the water where they have lived as larvae. They can survive until winter, and some adults hibernate. Males feed on nectar and other plant juices, but females need blood meals before they can lay their eggs. Mosquitoes have long mouthparts that they use to pierce skin (human or animal) and suck up blood. They are found near ponds, rivers and stagnant pools of water.

ACTUAL SIZE

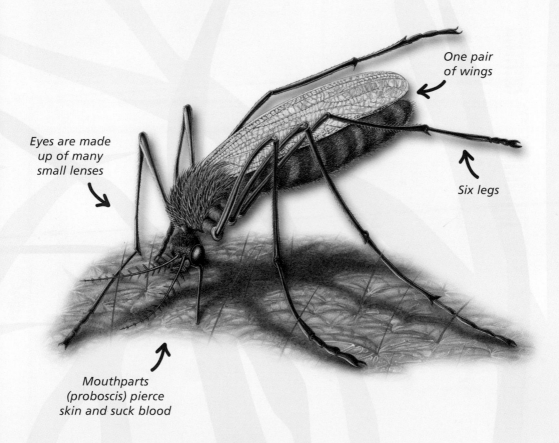

One pair
of wings

Six legs

Eyes are made
up of many
small lenses

Mouthparts
(proboscis) pierce
skin and suck blood

BUGS

FACT FILE

Scientific name *Inachis io*

Habitat Flowery gardens and meadows

Size 50–75 mm wingspan

Wings Two pairs

Breeding Larvae are called caterpillars

SUPER FACT

Peacock butterflies get their name from the large eyelike patterns on their wings, which are similar to the eye-shaped patterns on the tails of peacock birds.

PHOTO FILE

The butterfly bush, or buddleia, is a magnet to butterflies, particularly the peacock because the tiny flowers hold sweet-tasting nectar.

MY NOTES & PICTURES

I'VE SEEN... Feeding ◯   Flying ◯

PEACOCK BUTTERFLY

Welcome visitors to the garden, peacock butterflies are often seen on buddleia in summer. They wake from hibernation in spring and soon mate. Females lay small green eggs in batches of up to 500, often on nettles or hops, the caterpillars' favourite food. Adults emerge from the pupae in July and feed on nectar from flowers, or suck the juice from over-ripe fruit. The life expectancy of adults is one year.

ACTUAL SIZE

Two pairs of wings

Long antennae used for smelling and touching

Hair on thorax

Four false eyes on wings

Dark-brown wing edges

IN THE... Garden ◯   Park ◯   School field ◯

BUGS

FACT FILE

Scientific name *Vanessa atalanta*

Habitat Gardens and meadows

Size 60 mm wingspan

Wings Two pairs

Breeding Larvae are called caterpillars

SUPER FACT

The larvae of red admirals are normally dark and bristled, but the colour varies from green–grey to black with yellow lines on either side.

PHOTO FILE

Butterflies use their straw-like mouthpart, the proboscis, to suck nectar from flowers, such as buddleia or feed on rotting fruit.

MY NOTES & PICTURES

I'VE SEEN... Feeding ◯ Flying ◯

RED ADMIRAL BUTTERFLY

Named after their 'admirable' colours, these butterflies are easily recognized by their dark-coloured wings with red bands and white spots. They have hints of blue and black spots on their hind wings. Red admirals are fast, powerful flyers and – unusually for butterflies – may fly at night. These insects are found throughout the UK and Europe and inhabit gardens, parks, woodlands, seashores and mountains.

ACTUAL SIZE

Long antennae used for smelling and touching

Red bands on forewings

Red patches along the back of hind wings

Edges of wings lined with blue spots

IN THE... Garden ◯ Park ◯ School field ◯

BUGS

FACT FILE

Scientific name *Deroceras reticulatum*

Habitat Damp places, such as soil and under plants

Size 40–55 mm

Breeding Young are small slugs

SUPER FACT

When disturbed, slugs produce a liquid, called slime. It is used for protection, and to create a smooth surface for movement. It is sticky and swells when it absorbs water.

PHOTO FILE

Slugs usually come out at night, but you can tell when they have been near plants by their sticky slime trails.

MY NOTES & PICTURES

I'VE SEEN... Feeding ◯　　　Flying ◯

SLUG

Netted slugs are light brown or grey in colour and are one of the most frequent slug visitors to gardens. They are herbivorous and eat a wide range of plants, particularly those with tender, sweet leaves such as seedlings. The garden slug is bluish-black with a pale underside. It produces orangey-yellow slime and feeds on garden plants such as lettuces, seedlings and strawberries. They are unwelcome visitors to the garden because they destroy so many plants.

ACTUAL SIZE

Two pairs of feelers or tentacles

Area behind head is called the mantle

Grey or light brown body

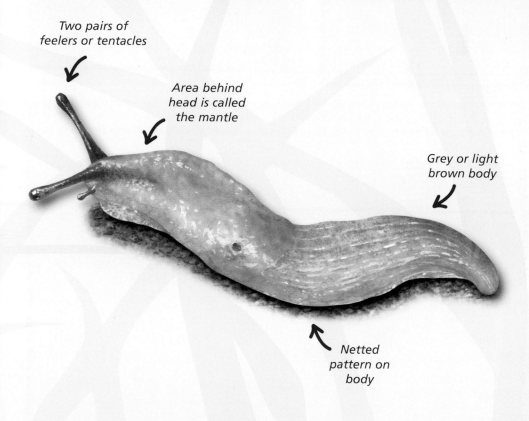

Netted pattern on body

IN THE... Garden ◯ Park ◯ School field ◯

BUGS

FACT FILE

Scientific name *Aglais urticae*

Habitat Flowery gardens and meadows

Size 40–55 mm wingspan

Wings Two pairs

Breeding Larvae are called caterpillars

SUPER FACT

Its Latin name, *Aglais urticae*, comes from the word for nettles, *urtica*, because this is the butterfly's favourite food.

PHOTO FILE

These insects rest with their wings closed, but rapidly open and close them to alarm predators with their bright colours.

MY NOTES & PICTURES

I'VE SEEN... Feeding ◯   Flying ◯

SMALL TORTOISESHELL

Named after their colouring, small tortoiseshells are often one of the first types of butterfly to be seen in spring. Adults emerge from hibernation in March or April and mate soon afterwards. They lay their eggs on food plants, such as nettles, and they hatch about ten days later. Small tortoiseshells are common butterflies and live in a range of habitats, particularly near human homes. They spend winter in sheds, garages and gardens.

ACTUAL SIZE

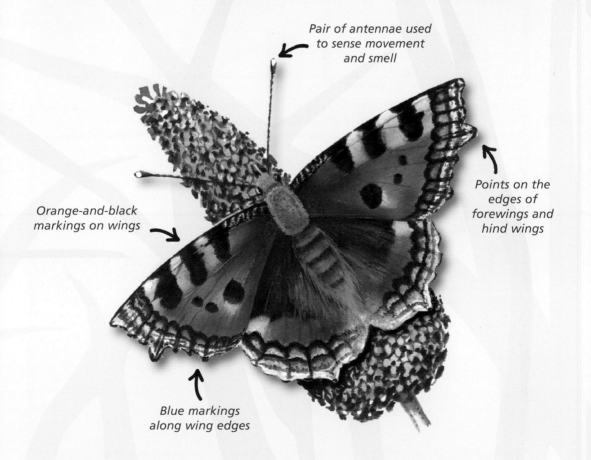

Pair of antennae used to sense movement and smell

Points on the edges of forewings and hind wings

Orange-and-black markings on wings

Blue markings along wing edges

IN THE... Garden ◯ Park ◯ School field ◯

FACT FILE

Scientific name *Helix aspersa*

Habitat Damp places, such as compost heaps

Size 25–40 mm

Wings None

Breeding Young are small snails

PHOTO FILE

Like slugs, snails leave slime trails. They eat plants using a rough mouthpart, called a radula, which scrapes and grazes food.

SUPER FACT

Snails belong to the same family as octopuses and squid – molluscs. These animals have soft bodies and no skeleton, although some molluscs have protective shells.

MY NOTES & PICTURES

I'VE SEEN... Feeding ◯ Flying ◯

SNAIL

Most snails live in water, but land snails are often found in gardens. Garden snails are quite large and have a brown or yellowy-brown shell with dark markings. They feed on plants, usually at night, when the soil is damp. Garlic snails are only 6–10 mm long and have glossy, dark-brown shells. They live in leaf litter and compost heaps, and eat fungi or rotting plants.

ACTUAL SIZE

Large, round shell patterned with brown and cream

Shell has up to five spirals

Two pairs of sensitive feelers, or tentacles

Soft body moves on a film of slime

BUGS

FACT FILE

Scientific name *Lucanus cervus*

Habitat Woodlands and gardens

Size 20–80 mm

Wings Two pairs

Breeding White larvae with brown heads

SUPER FACT

Stag beetles were once common in gardens and parklands, but they have become increasingly rare over the last 50 years and are now threatened with extinction.

PHOTO FILE

Eggs are laid in rotting wood. Larvae feed on wood for up to six years before they pupate. Adults emerge in summer.

MY NOTES & PICTURES

I'VE SEEN... Feeding ◯   Flying ◯

STAG BEETLE

One of the largest and most impressive insects, stag beetles can be heard as they noisily fly at dusk, searching for mates. Adults may only live for a few months and can survive without feeding. Males have large mouthparts, called mandibles, which they use to fight one another for females. Gardens with undisturbed areas of rotting wood may attract these endangered animals, as the larvae feed on wood.

ACTUAL SIZE

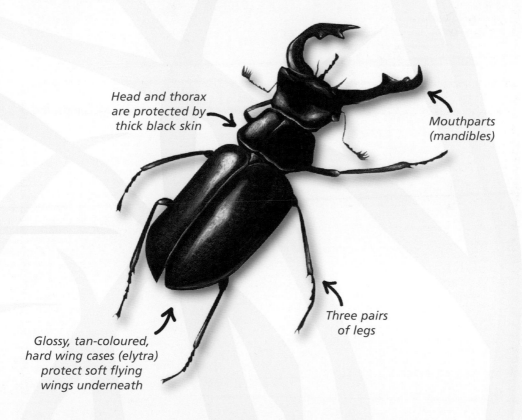

Head and thorax are protected by thick black skin

Mouthparts (mandibles)

Three pairs of legs

Glossy, tan-coloured, hard wing cases (elytra) protect soft flying wings underneath

IN THE... Garden ◯   Park ◯   School field ◯

BUGS

FACT FILE

Scientific name *Vespula vulgaris*

Habitat Gardens and woodlands

Size 10–14 mm

Wings Two pairs

Breeding Larvae grow in cells or 'combs'

SUPER FACT

Wasps belong to the same family of insects as bees and ants. Larvae feed on insects, and adults feed on nectar or other sugary substances, such as rotting fruit.

PHOTO FILE

There are more than 4000 types of social wasp around the world. They are closely related to bees, ants and sawflies.

MY NOTES & PICTURES

I'VE SEEN... Feeding ◯ Flying ◯

WASP

Common wasps live in large colonies and live in a large nest made out of chewed wood fibres. They often choose to nest near or in houses, and can become troublesome, since wasps can inflict painful stings. Queens are the only females that reproduce, and they come out of hibernation in spring ready to start a new colony. The first eggs she lays produce female workers, and later on her eggs produce males and new queens.

ACTUAL SIZE

Four small marks at back end of thorax

Wings are held along the length of the body

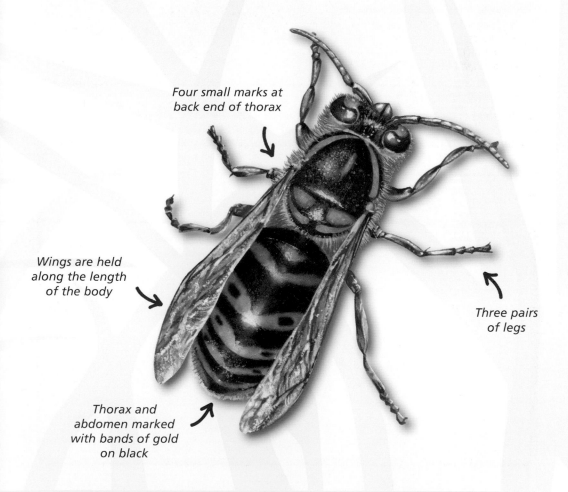

Three pairs of legs

Thorax and abdomen marked with bands of gold on black

IN THE... Garden ◯ Park ◯ School field ◯

FACT FILE

Scientific name *Aleyrodes* species

Habitat Farms and gardens

Size 1.5 mm

Wings Two pairs

Breeding Larvae are called nymphs

SUPER FACT

Whiteflies are attracted to yellow, so gardeners sometimes plant marigolds near their crops to encourage the whitefly to feed on them instead.

PHOTO FILE

Whiteflies leave a sticky sugary substance on leaves. It encourages the growth of sooty mould, which then damages plants.

MY NOTES & PICTURES

I'VE SEEN... Feeding ◯   Flying ◯

WHITEFLY

There are many different types of whitefly that attack garden plants, house plants and greenhouse plants. They lay their eggs on the leaves of their host plants and both the larvae and adults feed on sap, causing some damage but also passing viruses between plants. Tens of thousands of whitefly can live on a single tree or vegetable crop. They have a very short life cycle and can go from egg to adult in just three weeks.

ACTUAL SIZE

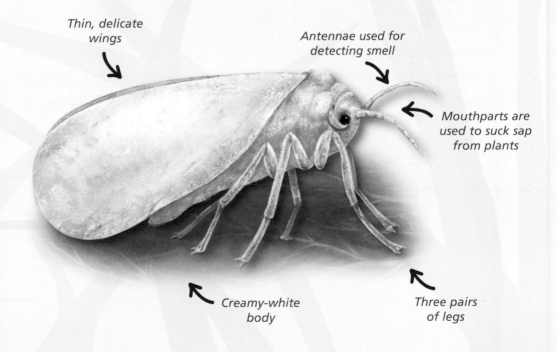

Thin, delicate wings

Antennae used for detecting smell

Mouthparts are used to suck sap from plants

Creamy-white body

Three pairs of legs

IN THE... Garden ◯ Park ◯ School field ◯

BUGS

FACT FILE

Scientific name *Oniscus asellus*

Habitat Soil and compost heaps

Size 13–16 mm

Wings None

Breeding Young are called stadia

SUPER FACT

Woodlice are not insects, but crustaceans, like shrimps and lobsters. Most crustaceans live in the oceans but woodlice can survive on land.

PHOTO FILE

Pill woodlice are able to coil up into balls. Their hard, glossy upperbody is like armour, and protects their softer body underneath.

MY NOTES & PICTURES

I'VE SEEN... Feeding ◯   Flying ◯

WOODLOUSE

Common creatures in a garden habitat, woodlice eat rotting material and use their senses of sight and smell to find food. Woodlice often eat in a group, under stones or vegetation, where they can hide from predators. When threatened, woodlice flatten their bodies and clamp themselves to a stone or wood. After mating, females carry their eggs in a special 'brood pouch' until they are ready to hatch.

ACTUAL SIZE

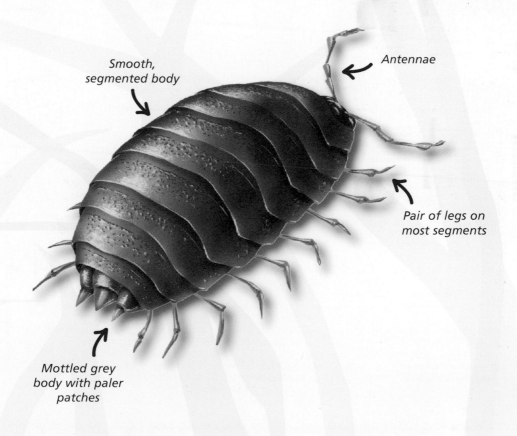

Smooth, segmented body

Antennae

Pair of legs on most segments

Mottled grey body with paler patches

GLOSSARY

Antennae A pair of long, sensitive structures on an insect's head.

Bush One plant with several woody branches, or a group of shrubs.

Camouflage The natural colouring of an animal that enables it to blend in with its environment.

Crown The spreading branches and leaves of a tree.

Deciduous Woody plants and trees that shed their leaves each year during autumn, with new leaves growing in spring.

Evergreen Plants and trees that keep their leaves all year round.

Juvenile Young animal.

Overwinter To remain alive through winter.

Pupate The process where a butterfly larva becomes a pupa.

Roost When animals, such as birds and bats, rest or sleep, or the name for a place where this happens.

ACKNOWLEDGEMENTS

The publisher would like to thank the following artists whose work appears in this book:
Ian Jackson, Mike Saunders

All other artworks are from MKP Archives

The publisher would like to thank the following picture sources whose photographs appear in this book:

Cover: Yellowj/Shutterstock

1 kesipun/Shutterstock; 3 David Dohnal/Shutterstock; 7(b) Graeme Lawton/Fotolia, (t) Jonathan Peat/Fotolia; 8 marilyna/Fotolia; 9(b) Cornelis Van Wessel/Fotolia, (t) Dave Timms/Fotolia; 10 Noah Strycker/Fotolia; 11(b) James Warren/Fotolia, (t) Sally Wallis/Fotolia; 12(b) Andrzej Tokarski/Fotolia, (m) khz/Fotolia, (t) Van Truan/Fotolia; 13(t) AndreasG/Fotolia, (b) Roger Wilmshurst/FLPA; 14(l) Iouri Timofeev/Fotolia, (r) Geza Farkas/Fotolia; 15 Nathalie Pecqueur/Fotolia; 16(b) Detlef Rother/Fotolia, (t) michael Jokrdan/Fotolia; 17 Joe & Mareike Alvarado/Fotolia; 18(b) Anneke Schram/Fotolia, (t) Otmar Smit/Fotolia; 19 Bernhard Weber/Fotolia; 20(l) Phaif/Fotolia, (r) Daiphoto/Fotolia; 21 Michel Gatti/Fotolia; 24 Richard Sheppard/Fotolia; 26 Denis Istomin/Fotolia; 28 Robert Ford/Fotolia; 30 zastavkin/Fotolia; 32 Sasha Radosavljevic/Fotolia; 34 Véronique El Youssfi/poret/Fotolia; 36 Anne Katrin Figge/Fotolia; 38 Candida Godson/Fotolia; 40 Peter Spiro/Fotolia; 42 marilyna/Fotolia; 44 torugo/Fotolia; 46 Sergey Chushkin/Fotolia; 48 Thomas Jacob/Fotolia; 50 Benoit Desveaux/Fotolia; 54 Freddy Smeets/Fotolia; 58 Graça Victoria/Fotolia; 64 David Marescaux/Fotolia; 66 Monique Pouzet/Fotolia; 68 edsweb/Fotolia; 74 Martina Berg/Fotolia; 76 Shane Kennedy/Fotolia; 78 Mike Lane/FLPA; 80 Tony Hamblin/FLPA; 82 Mike Lane/FLPA; 84 Walter Rohdich/FLPA; 88 Brian Lambert/Fotolia; 90 Anette Linnea Rasmussen/Fotolia; 92 Janusz Doboszynski/Fotolia; 94 Tomasz Kubis/Fotolia; 96 Martin B Withers/FLPA; 98 John Hawkins/FLPA; 100 Jacques Tournel/Fotolia; 102 marilyna/Fotolia; 104 imagepro/Fotolia; 106 Christophe Fouquin/Fotolia; 108 David Hosking/FLPA; 110 Kerioak/Fotolia; 112 Gregory Smellinckx/Fotolia; 114 Neil Bowman/FLPA; 116 Christophe Fouquin/Fotolia; 118 Kerry Wilkinson/Fotolia; 120 Christian Marx/Fotolia; 122 Mike Lane/FLPA; 124 Kerioak/Fotolia; 126 Andrzej Tokarski/Fotolia; 128 Pookini/Fotolia; 130 Frédéric Chausse/Fotolia; 132 Weston Palmer/Fotolia; 134 krismercer/Fotolia; 136 Luc Patureau/Fotolia; 140 Derek Middleton/FLPA; 142 marilyna/Fotolia; 144 Gregory Smellinckx/Fotolia; 148 Daniel Lewis/Fotolia; 150 XAO/Fotolia; 152 Phil McLean/FLPA; 154 B. Borrell Casals/FLPA; 156 Photolibrary Group Ltd; 160 Peter Bialas/Fotolia; 162 Ronnie Howard/Fotolia; 164 Ismael Montero/Fotolia; 166 Meinhard Gerstberger/Fotolia; 168 John Hayes/Fotolia; 170 Martina Berg/Fotolia; 172 Marco Koroll/Fotolia; 174 Sergey Chushkin/Fotolia; 176 Bine/Fotolia; 178 Nigel Cattlin/FLPA; 180 FLPA; 182 Saoirse Mac Cárthaigh/Fotolia; 184 Pawel Pietras/Fotolia; 186 Bob Gibbons/FLPA; 188 Photolibrary Group Ltd; 190 Heidi & Hans-Jurgen Koch/Minden Pictures/FLPA; 194 Hazel Proudlove/Fotolia; 198 Dave Massey/Fotolia; 198 Henryk Dybka/Fotolia; 200 Martina Moser/Fotolia; 202 Alwyn J Roberts/FLPA; 204 Christophe Fouquin/Fotolia; 206 Anette Linnea Rasmussen/Fotolia; 208 criber/Fotolia; 210 Alison Bowden/Fotolia; 214 Jp Nel/Fotolia; 216 AZ-/Fotolia; 218 Lucy Clark/Fotolia; 220 Nigel Cattlin/FLPA; 222 B. Borrell Casals/FLPA

All other photographs from:
digitalSTOCK, digitalvision, Dreamstime.com, Fotolia.com, iStockphoto.com, John Foxx, PhotoAlto, PhotoDisc, PhotoEssentials, PhotoPro, Stockbyte